Cracking the

1st Grade

Reading & Math

A Parent's Guide to Helping Your Child Excel in School

By Mary Austin, Sarah Little,
and the Staff of The Princeton Review

Random House, Inc.
New York

RandomHouse.com

The Princeton Review is one of the nation's leaders in test preparation and a pioneer in the world of education. The Princeton Review offers a broad range of products and services to measurably improve academic performance for millions of students every year.

The Princeton Review is not affiliated with Princeton University or Educational Testing Service.

The Princeton Review, Inc.
2315 Broadway
New York, NY 10024
E-mail: booksupport@review.com

Published in the United States by Random House, Inc., New York

ISBN: 978-0-375-76602-2

Printed in the United States of America

9 8 7 6 5 4 3 2 1

First Edition

CREDITS

Series Editor: Casey Cornelius

Content Editor: Roni Menachem

Development Editor: Sherine Gilmour

Production Editor: Melissa Lewis

Art Director: Neil McMahon

Senior Designer: Doug McGredy

Production Manager: Greta Blau

Production Coordinator: Leif Osgood

Illustrators: Doug McGredy, Tom Racine, and Tim Goldman

ACKNOWLEDGMENTS

This book would not have been possible without the contributions of a talented team of writers, editors, artists, and developers, who tackled this series with devotion and smarts.

CONTENTS

147 MATH

Introduction

You and Your Kid

Your job is to help your child excel in school. Everyone agrees that children bloom when their parents, family, friends, and neighbors nudge them to learn—from the Department of Education to the Parent Teacher Association, from research organizations known as "educational laboratories" to the local newspaper, from the National Endowment for the Arts to kids' shows on TV.

But state standards hardly make for enjoyable leisure reading, and plowing through reports on the best ways to teach math and reading can leave you with a headache rubbing your temples. You're caught in the middle: you want to help your kid, but it's not always easy to know how.

That's where *Cracking the First Grade* comes in. We identified the core skills that first graders need to know. Then, we put them together along with some helpful tips for you and fun activities for your kid. We built this book to be user friendly, so you and your kid can fit in some quality time, even as you're juggling all your other parental responsibilities.

A Parent's Many Hats

As a parent, you're a cook, a chauffeur, a coach, an ally, and oh so many other things. So, keep it simple. Check out these ways you can use *Ahead of the Curve* to get involved in your child's academic life.

Teacher. You taught your kid how to cross the street and tie his or her shoes. In addition, you may have worked to teach your child academic skills by reviewing the alphabet, helping your child memorize facts, and explaining concepts to your child. By doing so, you are modeling a great learning attitude and great study habits for your child. You are teaching him or her the value of school.

Nurturer. As a nurturer, you're always there to support your child through tough times, celebrate your child's successes, and give your child rules and limits. You encourage your child while holding high expectations. All of this can help your child feel safe and supported enough to face challenges and opportunities at school, like new classmates, new teachers, and so on.

Intermediary. You're your child's first representative in the world. You're the main go-between and communicator for your child (school-to-home and home-to-school).

Advocate. As an advocate, you can do many things: sit on advisory councils at school, assist in the classroom, join the PTA, volunteer in school programs, vote in school board elections, and argue for learning standards and approaches you believe in.

. . . .

Sometimes it's hard to know what to do, and it's easy to feel overwhelmed. But remember, it's not all on your shoulders. Research shows that family and close friends all have a huge effect on kids' academic success.

What's in This Book

The Skill
Each lesson targets a key first-grade skill. You and your kid can either work on all the lessons or pick and choose the lessons you want. If time is short, your kid can work on an activity without reviewing an entire lesson.

Just for You
Tips, advice, insight, and clues from parents and educators start here! Read this before diving into the rest of the lesson.

First Things First
This is the starting point for your kid in every lesson.

Supplies
Get your kid in the habit of gathering supplies before starting a lesson.

Jump Right In!
These are questions for your kid to complete independently. Give your kid as much time as he or she needs. But if your kid takes more than 30 minutes, consider the possibility that he or she may be having a hard time focusing, be unfamiliar with the skill, or have difficulty with the skill.

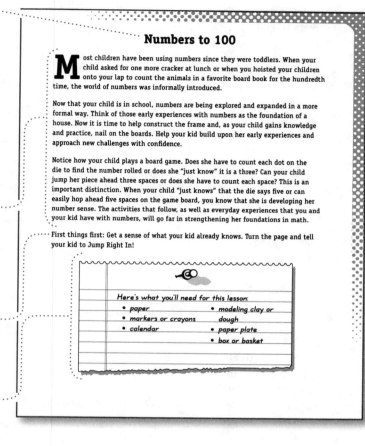

Numbers to 100

Most children have been using numbers since they were toddlers. When your child asked for one more cracker at lunch or when you hoisted your children onto your lap to count the animals in a favorite board book for the hundredth time, the world of numbers was informally introduced.

Now that your child is in school, numbers are being explored and expanded in a more formal way. Think of those early experiences with numbers as the foundation of a house. Now it is time to help construct the frame and, as your child gains knowledge and practice, nail on the boards. Help your kid build upon her early experiences and approach new challenges with confidence.

Notice how your child plays a board game. Does she have to count each dot on the die to find the number rolled or does she "just know" it is a three? Can your child jump her piece ahead three spaces or does she have to count each space? This is an important distinction. When your child "just knows" that the die says five or can easily hop ahead five spaces on the game board, you know that she is developing her number sense. The activities that follow, as well as everyday experiences that you and your kid have with numbers, will go far in strengthening her foundations in math.

First things first: Get a sense of what your kid already knows. Turn the page and tell your kid to Jump Right In!

Here's what you'll need for this lesson:
- paper
- markers or crayons
- calendar
- modeling clay or dough
- paper plate
- box or basket

Feel free to read the questions aloud.

Jump Right In!

1. Which picture shows a pattern?

A. ○ □ △ □   C. △ ⌐

Checking In
Check your kid's answers to the Jump Right In! questions. Whether your kid aced the Jump Right In! questions or had some trouble, here's stuff you can do to keep supporting your kid

Checking In

❶ Answers for page 13:

1. A

2. C

3. An A+ answer: "Primates are animals such as apes, gorillas, and mo The story says that these animals are examples of primates and tha their hands and feet to hold on to things."

4. An A+ answer: "Aquatic means something that lives in the water. T says that fish and turtles are aquatic animals that live in the water

Did your child get the correct answers? If so, ask your child to point out the clues in the story that showed the meaning of the words *watch* and *sign*.

Did your child get one of the answers wrong? If so, explain to your child that *watch* and *sign* have more than one meaning. Review the answer choices to q and 2 and talk about the various meanings of the words *watch* and *sign*.

Watch Out!

Sometimes third graders try to figure out a word's meaning by using the det find the most interesting. For example, did your child select the wrong mea word "watch" in question 1? Maybe he or she was thinking about watchi

Watch Out!
These tips identify common pitfalls and help you help your child avoid them.

What to Know...
Review these key skills, definitions, and examples with your kid. Questions and tips are provided so you and your kid can talk about the skills.

What to Know...

Your child is learning how addition and subtraction relate to each other by related facts and writing fact families.

Review these skills with your child this way:

- **Related addition facts** are a pair of addition facts that use the sam numbers. (Your child might use the term *turn-around facts*.)
- **Related subtraction facts** are a pair of subtraction facts that use three numbers.
- An addition and subtraction **fact family** is a group of two additional two subtraction facts that use the same three numbers.

First Graders Are...
Your child's natural stages of growth can play into academic success. These tips give you insider info on the developmental stages of your child and how to help your child through his or her transitions.

First Graders Are...

Children of this age group are beginning to think abstractly, but they still need to relate w they learn to the concrete wo

On Your Way to an "A"
Fun, educational activities your kid can do with you, family, neighbors, babysitters, and friends at home, in the car, during errands—anywhere.

Your child can practice working with shapes with these activities. You to read these activities aloud to your child.

On Your Way to an "A" Activities

{30 minutes}

Type: Arts and Crafts
Materials needed: washable paint, construction paper, plastic plates
Number of players: 2 or more

Wear an old shirt or smock. Put some paint on a pl Find different-shaped objects around your house t used as stamps. Dip the object in the paint and sta paper. Some examples include a cut cucumber or p bottom of a box, or the bottom of a cheese triangle painting is dry, write the name of each shape you

Study Right
Who hasn't heard that study skills can make or break a student? Check out these tips for study skills your kid can apply immediately.

👍 *Study Right*

Help your child make a book of shapes. Staple several pieces of pape top of each page write the name of a shape. Ask your child to search magazine to find examples of that sha

Web Site Help
Check out this Web site. Whether your kid needs more practice on this skill or wants to venture forth into other skills, there are resources here for you!

Has your child breezed through the activities? If so, he or she can work Your Head activity independently. If not, look for help with sequencing www.princetonreviw.com/book. You'll probably want to read the activit your child.

Using Your Head

{15 minutes}

*Grab a **pencil**!*

Read the next part of the story "The Pet Shop" belo draw pictures to show the order of what happened

Using Your Head
If your kid feels confident, here's an independent, challenging activity where your kid can show off what he or she knows.

How Does Your Kid Learn Best?

Did you know that your kid learns in a lot of different ways? When kids learn, they use their minds, their bodies, and their senses—their sense of sight, sound, taste, touch, and smell.

Some kids can succeed in any classroom while others need specialized learning support, but all of them have strengths and weaknesses. Your kid can learn to rely on his or her strengths and then work on any weaknesses. This book is full of activities that address each of these learning styles.

Visually—Using Our Sense of Sight
Your kid may learn best by looking at pictures, outlines, maps, and such. Your kid may like to draw pictures or take notes.

Auditory—Using Our Sense of Sound
Your kid may learn best by listening to teachers speak, discussing with friends and classmates, and listening to music while studying. Your kid may like to tap a rhythm with his or her pen or pencil while studying.

Kinesthetic—Using Our Sense of Touch and Movement
Your kid may learn best by moving, taking action, or walking around.

How to Use Learning Styles

Talk with your child about his or her successes at school, home, or with hobbies. How did your child learn what he or she needed to succeed? Does your child prefer to learn a certain way? Knowing how your child learns best can help you make the most of your child's natural strengths and work on his or her weaknesses.

Right now, while your child is young, he or she may not have a clear learning style. That's okay. Encourage your child to try different learning methods that work. In the long run, this will help your child become a well-rounded learner!

Want to Know More?

Check out these Web sites and organizations for more reading and math support.

Family Math and Matemática Para La Familia. If you want information about more effectively helping your child in mathematics, go to http://equals.lhs.berkeley.edu/.

MAPPS (Math and Parent Partnerships). If you want activities and mini-courses to learn about becoming more engaged in your child's school mathematics program, go to http://math.arizona.edu/~mapps/.

Parents for Public Schools. If you want to find out about chapters of parents working together to advocate for school improvement, go to www.parents4publicschools.com.

Parent Training and Information Centers. If you want to find out about education and services to assist a child with disabilities, go to www.taalliance.org/centers/index.htm.

PESA (Parent Expectations Support Achievement). If you want techniques for improving your child's academic achievement, go to http://streamer.lacoe.edu/pesa/.

PIQE (Parent Institute for Quality Education). If you want to learn about how to motivate your child in school, develop a home learning environment, work with the school system, or prepare for college, go to www.pique.org.

Reading Is Fundamental. If you want help with supporting your child's reading and learning, go to www.rif.org.

A Quick Guide to the Reading Lessons—Pronunciation Key

The reading lessons in the book address a range of skills, from phonics and word work skills to reading comprehension skills. The first six reading lessons focus on phonics and word work skills.

Anytime a sound in a word is written as it should be pronounced (rather than as it is spelled), you will see the sound sandwiched in backslashes. For example, with the word "cat," the 'c' is not pronounced "see"—the 'c' in "cat" is pronounced like a 'k.' Therefore, when you and your child need to emphasize how to pronounce the 'c' in "cat," you will see the word "cat" written as \k\at.

To help you guide your child correctly, we've noted how these sounds should be pronounced in the lessons. Here's a guide to what we're talking about.

\ă\	mat, map, mad, gag, ...	\m\	me, murmer, swim, ...
\ā\	day, fade, date, drape, ...	\n\	now, own, near, dinner, ...
\b\	baby, bean, bring, ...	\ŏ\	mom, job, cop, octopus, ...
\ch\	chin, choose, cheese, cherry, ...	\ō\	bone, know, go, row, ...
\d\	did, add, dear, glad, ...	\p\	prank, pepper, lip, peas, ...
\ĕ\	bet, pet, bed, peck, ...	\r\	red, aardvark, beard, car, ...
\ē\	easy, mealy...	\s\	see, less, source, sleek, ...
\f\	feather, father, fifty, taffy, ...	\sh\	shy, mission, machine, ...
\g\	go, gift, big, leg, ...	\t\	tie, better, late, meet, ...
\h\	hat, ahead, hardy, ...	\ŭ\	cut, up, jump, run, ...
\ĭ\	tip, banish, active, lip, ...	\ū\	cute, mule, use, fuel, ...
\ī\	site, side, buy, fry, ...	\v\	vivid, veer, very, over, ...
\j\	job, gem, join, judge, ...	\w\	wow, away, we, ...
\k\	kin, cook, ache, keep, ...	\y\	yard, young, yet, yes, ...
\l\	lily, lamb, pool, play, ...	\z\	zoo, raise, blaze, ...

Developing Awareness of Sounds

Teachers and researchers have spent countless hours trying to figure out the best ways to teach kids how to read. They've spent years debating. Laws have been passed. Laws have been changed. And the debate and research go on.

You don't have to be a reading researcher to help your child learn how to read. You can read to him or her. You can also make sure your kid has a ton of interesting books. But you might find it helpful to find out about some popular techniques for working with sounds and letters. For example, researchers use the terms and phrases "blending onset and rime" (saying certain sounds in a word together) and "segmenting phonemes" (breaking apart the sounds in a word). You probably won't use these terms around the house. But in this lesson, you'll get a few examples of what these terms mean and how to use these techniques to help your kid read.

Here's what you'll need for this lesson:
- *family photos or children's books*
- *a large piece of paper*
- *scissors*
- *glue or tape*
- *5 pennies*
- *markers or crayons*

What to Know...

You and your kid can count syllables, blend onset and rime, blend phonemes, segment phonemes, and manipulate phonemes. Wow! That's a mouthful. To keep it simple, we've reviewed each of these skills in a clear, direct way.

Counting syllables

- A **syllable** is a unit of spoken language pronounced with a single uninterrupted sounding of the voice. A syllable can be made up of a single vowel or a vowel sound grouped with one or more consonants.

Counting syllables helps your kid pronounce words. Breaking down a long word into syllables helps your child hear all of the word parts. Once he hears the word parts, he'll have an easier time saying the entire word. Counting syllables also comes in handy when your kid is reading unfamiliar words. Reading the word *fantastic* can seem a bit overwhelming to a first grader, but if he learns to break the word down into smaller parts, it doesn't seem as daunting.

Ask your child to clap out the syllables in a word and then count the syllables. For example:

Parent: "Let's clap out the word *fantastic*."
Child: (while clapping): "Fan–tas–tic."
Parent: "How many syllables?"
Child: "Three."

Practice clapping syllables with your child. Try to work with a range of syllables (from one-syllable words to four-syllable words). Here are some words you can use: *ta-ble, pi-a-no, pen-cil, mag-ni-fi-cent, en-er-gy, mi-cro-wave, trum-pet.* (These words are shown with their syllable breaks.)

 *Checking In*

How did your child do with counting syllables? If your child is having difficulty, clap out the word first, and then ask her to clap the same word. If clapping syllables seemed easy for your child and you didn't have to model at all, challenge her to think of words with a given number of syllables. For example, ask your child: "Can you think of a word with two syllables?"

Watch Out!

First graders may sometimes pronounce words incorrectly, which makes it more difficult to separate the syllables. For example, when counting the syllables in the word *bed,* you may hear your child stretch the vowel and say: "buh – eehhh – dd," making it sound like three syllables instead of one syllable. You can help your child by saying each word crisply when modeling examples.

Blending Onset and Rime

- **Oral blending** is putting sounds together to form a word. This can help your kid to understand how sounds are combined to make words.

- An **onset sound** is the sound at the beginning of a syllable, and the **rime** is the rest of the syllable. For example, in the word *bat,* the /b/ is the onset and the –at is the rime (the vowel always goes with the rime).

  NOTE: Sounds are represented in this book with slashes on either side of the sound (the sound for *b* in *ball*: /b/, the sound for *ch* in *chair*: /ch/). See page 8 for more help with how sounds are represented.

- **Onset and rime blending** is putting the spoken onset and rime together to form a word.

Review these skills with your child. Remember to say the sounds, not the letters.

Parent:	"/b/ ... at. What's the word?"
Child:	"Bat."
Parent:	"/ch/ ... air. What's the word?"
Child:	"Chair."

Checking In

Was your child able to hear the onset and rime and put them together? If not, stick to small sound segments like /b/–at and /c/–at. This will help your child get used to putting these parts together and understanding that words can be broken into parts. If /b/–at and /c/–at are too easy, then switch to words with more complex sound segments, like /t//r/–ip (sound out /t/, sound out /r/, sound out -ip), /s/l/–ip, and /f// l/–ip. With these more complex sounds, kids have to put more than one letter sound in the onset.

Blending Phonemes

- A **phoneme** is a distinct unit of sound. **Phoneme blending** is putting these distinct sounds together to create words.

Review this skill with your child. Remember to say the sounds, not the letters.

> Parent: "/p/ ... /ĭ/ ... /n/. What's the word?"
> Child: "Pin."

 *Watch Out!*

In first grade, children are developing their awareness of sounds and may confuse phonemes that sound similar, such as /b/ and /p/. Have you ever heard your kid say *botato* instead of *potato*? Make sure to pronounce words and sounds carefully so that your child will be able to pick out the sounds of the words.

Segmenting Phonemes

- **Segmentation** means breaking up words into sounds. You can think of it as the opposite of blending.
- **Segmentation by phonemes** means breaking up words by distinct units of sounds.

Review this skill with your child. Remember to say the sounds, not the letters.

> Parent: "Can you chop up the word *cat* to find its sounds?"
> Child: "/k/ ... /ă/ ... /t/."

Checking In

Some kids get this right away and will say, "That's easy!" If so, try words with more sounds:

> Parent: "Say all the sounds in the words *glass*."
> Child: "/g/ ... /l/ ... /ă/ ... /s/."
> Parent: "Listen to the word *spend*. Now say all the sounds you hear."
> Child: "/s/ ... /p/ ... /ĕ/ ... /n/ ... /d/."

Your child may already be learning about which sounds belong to each letter. When your child starts writing, she will most likely stretch out a word to hear its phonemes, and write down the corresponding letters. So, segmenting phonemes is a necessary skill for beginning writing!

 *Watch Out!*

In order to have segmenting down, your child will have to be able to sequence sounds properly. Many first graders, when asked to segment *cat,* will say the following: "/t/ ... /a/ ... /k/." This is perfectly normal because kids often remember the last sound in the word and say the last sound first. Encourage your child to try again, starting with the first sound he or she hears.

Manipulating Phonemes

- **Phoneme manipulation** means to omit or substitute sounds to make new words.

Review this skill with your child. Remember to say the sound, not the letter.

Parent: "What word would you have if you changed the /t/ in *Tommy* to an /m/?"
Child: "Mommy."
Parent: "What word would you have if you changed the /p/ at the end of *cup* to a /t/?"
Child: "Cut."
Parent: "What word would you have if you left out the /p/ in the middle of *spend*?"
Child: "Send."

 *Watch Out!*

Vowels can be tough sounds for first graders to hear and say because they often have so many different types of sounds. Think about the letter *a* in *apple, ape,* and *art*. Make sure to enunciate the correct vowel sound very clearly. See page 8 for more information on the pronunciation of different sounds.

You and your child can practice phonological awareness with these activities.

On Your Way to an "A" Activities

20 minutes

Type: Arts and Crafts
Materials needed: markers or crayons, glue or tape, family photos or a few of your child's favorite books, 1 large piece of paper
Number of players: 2

Help your child make a "Syllable Name Sort." Take a large piece of paper and make four columns labeled "1," "2," "3," and "4 or more." With your child, look at photos of your family or at your child's favorite books. Say aloud the names of your family members or the characters in the books one at a time. Have your child clap out the syllables in the names. If the name has one syllable, your child will draw a picture of the family member or character in the "1" column; if the name has two syllables, he or she will be drawn in the "2" column; and so on. (If you have extra copies of pictures, your child could also cut out the faces and glue or tape them in the appropriate column to make a syllable collage.) Try to clap out the names of 8–10 family members or characters to provide a good variety.

10 minutes

Type: Speaking and Listening
Materials needed: none
Number of players: 2

Play "Row, Row, Row Your Roat" to help your child get comfortable with different sounds. In this activity, you will sing different versions of "Row, Row, Row Your Boat." For each version, call out a different sound that will begin each *main* word. Sing the traditional version first, then call out a sound and change the beginning sound of each of the main words. For example, if you called out /s/, the song would change to: "Sow, sow, sow your soat sently sown the stream. Serrily, serrily, serrily, serrily, sife is but a seam." This activity gets very silly and is guaranteed to make your kid giggle.

Type: Speaking and Listening
Materials needed: paper, pencil, 5 pennies
Number of players: 2

{15 minutes}

This is called "Push the Pennies," and it helps your child practice phoneme segmentation. In this activity, you will draw three boxes on a piece of paper. One box will have two spaces, one will have three spaces, and one will have four spaces (see example below). You will then say a word slowly to your child and tell him or her how many sounds the word has (it should have two to four phonemes). Your child will then push the pennies into each box as he or she says the phonemes. For example, you can say the word *pen* and tell your child that it has three sounds. Your child then takes three pennies and pushes the pennies, one at a time, into the box with three spaces as he or she says each sound: /p/ ... /e/ ... /n/. You will probably have to do a couple of examples to show your kid how to push the pennies.

Here are some examples of words:

Two phonemes: *at, in, it, is, on, my*

Three phonemes: *cat, hop, ten, pig, jet*

Four phonemes: *jump, flag, tent, clip*

Here's what the boxes should look like:

Has your child breezed through the activities? If so, he or she can work on this Using Your Head activity independently. You'll probably want to read the activity below aloud to your child.

Using Your Head

*Grab a **pencil** and some **crayons**!*

You get to go on a Syllable Scavenger Hunt! Look around your house for objects. Count the syllables in each object's name. Draw a picture, or try writing the object's name in the correct column.

1 syllable	2 syllables	3 syllables	4 syllables

Cracking the First Grade

Letters and Sounds

You know that your kid needs to learn the alphabet before she can to learn to read. But the letters of the alphabet can be tricky for kids. Just think about the letter *b*. If you flip it one way, it becomes a *d*. If you flip it another way, it becomes a *p*. What about the letter *a*? It may be easier to recognize but more difficult to know its sound. Consider the different sounds it makes in the following words: *ask, ape, about, watch*. Just think about how mind-boggling they must be for a first grader. However, being able to recognize all of the letters in the alphabet and knowing their corresponding sounds will eventually lead your child to become a reader. Once your child can quickly name a letter and its sound, she has the tools she needs to sound out words.

First things first: Get a sense of what your kid already knows. Turn the page and tell your kid to Jump Right In!

Here's what you'll need for this lesson:
- scissors
- glue or tape
- magazines or newspapers
- 26 sheets of paper
- note cards
- stapler
- timer
- baking dish
- sand or sugar

Feel free to read the questions aloud.

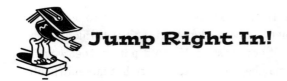

Jump Right In!

1. Match each letter with a picture that starts with the same sound.

2. Match each vowel with a picture.

3. Match the letters with a picture that starts with the same sound.

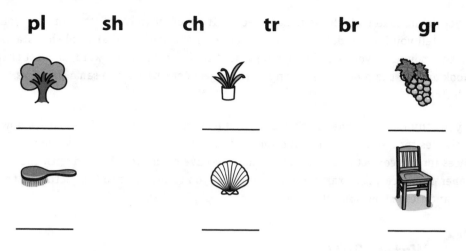

pl   sh   ch   tr   br   gr

_____   _____   _____

_____   _____   _____

4. Draw an animal that starts with a "t."

Excellent Job!

Checking In

Did your child match all the sounds correctly? If so, point to each letter and ask your child to tell you its sound. Then, ask your child to think of another word that starts with that sound. If your child is having a hard time thinking of a word, suggest that he look around the room to see if any of the objects start with the same sound as the letter.

Did your child match some of the sounds and pictures incorrectly? If so, narrow down the choices for her. Go to a mistake she made and say, "Try again. I'll give you two choices for the correct answer." Your child may have been overwhelmed with the number of choices. For example, for question 3, you could point to the picture of the plant and then show your child only two choices: *pl* and *sh*.

Watch Out!

It's very common for first graders to be confused by letter combinations. Some letter combinations are made up of two sounds that blend together. For example, in the word *plant,* the letters *pl* present a sound containing both /p/ and /l/. The confusing part is that some letter combinations create a brand-new sound, such as *ch* and *sh*. Sometimes your child may try to blend the *c* and *h* instead of treating *ch* as an individual sound. Provide several examples that start with the /ch/ sound and /sh/ sound so that your child can gain familiarity with these new sounds. Examples include: *chair, chin, chest, chips, chicken, ship, shout, shell, shark,* and *shoe.*

What to Know...

Here are some brief definitions with examples to review with your child:

- A blend is a sound represented by two or more consecutive consonants that run together when pronounced, such as *str, fl, br,* and *sk.*

To practice saying blends, have your child replace the beginning letter of a word with a blend. For example,

Parent: "Think about the word *cat*. Let's change the *c* to *fl*." (Write the letters *fl* for your child to see.) "What word would we have?"

Child: "Flat."

- A digraph is two letters that represent one speech sound, as *ch* for /ch/ in *chair, sh* for /sh/ in *shirt,* and *th* for /th/ in *thick.*

To practice with digraphs, have your child replace the beginning letter of a word with a digraph. For example,

Parent: "What would happen if we added *s* to the beginning of *hop*?" (Write the letters *sh* for your child to see.) "What word would we have?"

Child: "Shop."

- Long vowels are the vowel sounds in English that are also the names of the alphabet letters *a, e, i, o,* and *u,* as /ā/ in *paper,* /ē/ in *be,* /ī/ in *find,* /ō/ in *hope,* and /ū/ in *unicorn.*

- Short vowels are the sound qualities of /ă/, /ĕ/, /ĭ/, /ŏ/, and /ŭ/ heard in *pat, pet, pit, pot,* and *putt.*

To give your kid practice pronouncing long and short vowels, write two sets of vowels in two rows on a piece of paper. Write the first set in your regular handwriting; these will be the short vowels. Write elongated letters for the second set; these will be the long vowels. The elongated letters will help your child remember that the long vowels make a long vowel sound, and that they are different from the short vowels. Point to the short *a* and say, "Short *a* says /ă/, /ă/, /ă/, as in *pat*." Point to the long *a* and say, "Long *a* says /ā/, as in *paper*"—and really stretch out the long vowel sound. Repeat for each vowel and have your child say it with you.

On Your Way to an "A" Activities

{ 15 minutes }
Type: Active
Materials needed: none
Number of players: 3 or more

It's time to play Alphabet Freeze Tag! If you are the tagger, call out a letter from the alphabet. When one of the players is tagged by you, that player must freeze. The only way to become unfrozen is if the player can think of a word that starts with the letter you called. For example, if you are the tagger and call out "r," the person you tag can call out "rock," and then he or she is unfrozen. Keep playing, changing the letter every so often.

{ 10 minutes }
Type: Game/Competitive
Materials needed: none
Number of players: 2 or more

In this version of "I Spy," players will give clues about objects using the letters or sounds in the word. For example, if you were trying to get the other player to guess *desk,* you could use clues like "I spy with my little eye something that starts with the letter *d.*" A second clue could be "I spy with my little eye something that ends with /s//k/. The other player can ask you questions about the object like "Does it have a short *e* sound?" and you can answer yes or no. Make sure to take turns giving clues and asking questions.

You can work with your child on letters and their sounds using these activities.

Type: Game/Competitive

Materials needed: a set of note cards with the letters of the alphabet written on them (one letter on each card) and a timer

Number of players: 2

In "Grab It!" you will tell your child a word, and she will grab the letter that the word begins with. Spread out the alphabet cards on a table. Make sure they're not in order. It's important for first graders to recognize letters out of sequence. Start the timer and then call out a word. After your child finds the letter card that makes the beginning sound, continue calling out words for each letter of the alphabet. When all of the letter cards have been used and the game is over, stop the timer. Try the entire activity again and see if your child can beat her time.

Type: Reading/Writing

Materials needed: shallow baking dish, sand or sugar

Number of players: 2

For this activity, fill a shallow baking dish with about one-fourth of an inch of sand or sugar. Call out random words. Tell your child to use his finger in the sand or sugar to write the letter(s) of the sound he hears at the beginning of a word. The sensation of writing the letters in the sand or sugar will create a tactile association with the letters and their sounds. If you want to challenge your child, ask him to write the letter for the sound he hears at the end of the word.

First Graders Are...

Competitiveness is huge in first grade. Be prepared for your child to perhaps get upset if she can't guess the "I Spy" object or if she can't beat her fastest time in "Grab It!" If you find your child getting frustrated, let her give the clues in "I Spy," and get rid of the timer in "Grab It!"

Has your child breezed through the activities? If so, he or she can work on this Using Your Head activity independently. You'll probably want to read the activity below aloud to your child.

Using Your Head

Grab some **magazines** or **newspapers, scissors, glue** or **tape,** and **26 sheets of clean paper stapled together**!

You will create your very own Alphabet Book! Ask someone to help you make a book of 26 sheets of paper. Write one letter of the alphabet on the top of each page, starting with "A." Next, use magazines and newspapers to find pictures of things that start with each letter. Cut them out and glue or tape them in your book!

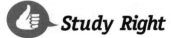 *Study Right*

It may take your kid a while to complete the Alphabet Book, but once she's finished, it can be used whenever you're helping your child read. For example, while reading, if your child is stuck on a word that contains the letter *b,* you can point to pictures on the "B" page in her dictionary to help her remember the sound. For an extra bonus, add sheets to the dictionary for digraphs. Go back to page 23 for more information on digraphs.

Rhyme and Spelling Patterns

I f you've read *The Cat in the Hat,* you probably were impressed by the way Dr. Seuss connects with kids and keeps them entertained for hours and hours. It's amazing how even the youngest child becomes enthralled by the musical rhythm of these rhyming books. What often goes unnoticed is that the rhymes in these silly books are helping your kid become a successful reader.

You might catch your child repeating phrases from *The Cat in the Hat,* or better yet, you might hear him coming up with his own rhymes. This rhyming ability shows that your child knows how to manipulate sounds. For example, he can replace the /k/ in *car* with a /f/ to make the word *far.* Research has shown that kids who are able to master this skill are more successful in beginning reading. Once your child sees rhyming words in print, he will begin to notice common spelling patterns and word families. Becoming familiar with spelling patterns will also help your child become a reading star. Once he knows and can identify the *ick* sound, reading *sick, tick, Rick,* and *trick* becomes much easier.

First things first: Get a sense of what your kid already knows. Turn the page and tell your kid to Jump Right In!

Here's what you'll need for this lesson:
- *paper*
- *markers or crayons*
- *book of nursery rhymes*
- *20 note cards*

Jump Right In!

Choose the object that rhymes with the picture.

1.

A.   B.   C.

2.

A.   B.   C.

3.

 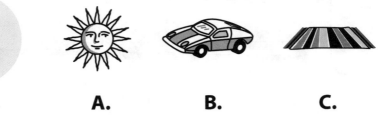

A.   B.   C.

4.

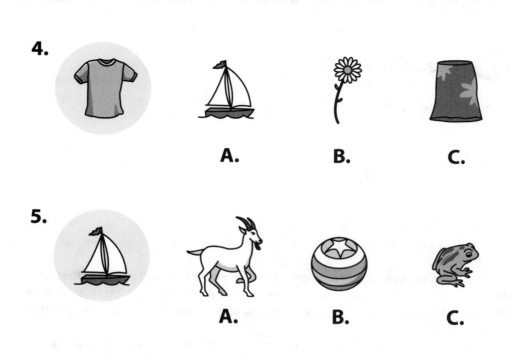

A.   B.   C.

5.

A.   B.   C.

6. Write 3 more words for the –**all** family.

call, ball, _____, _____, _____

7. Write 3 more words for the –**ug** family.

bug, dug, _____, _____, _____

Excellent Job!

Checking In

1. A
2. C
3. B
4. C
5. A
6. An A+ answer: (any of the following) tall, wall, mall, small, hall
7. An A+ answer: (any of the following) hug, jug, mug, rug, tug, slug, plug

Did your child get the correct answers? If so, ask your child to give you additional rhyming words. For example, point to question 1 and ask, "Can you think of another word that rhymes with *cat*?" Use the same line of questioning for the other questions.

Did your child get any of the answers wrong? If so, she may have been choosing objects with the same *beginning* sound. Remind your child that words that rhyme have the same *final* sounds. Help your child by saying each answer choice with the target word. Tell your child to pay attention to the way your mouth moves as you say each pair of words. Ask her to identify when your mouth moves the same way.

Watch Out!

When creating word families, your child might choose a word that rhymes but has a different spelling. For example, your child may suggest the word *crawl* for the *–all* family. Praise your child for identifying a word that rhymes with the other words in the *–all* family, but show your child that it doesn't belong in the *–all* family because it has a different spelling. Write the word *ball* and the word *crawl* and have your child notice the difference. *Crawl* is part of the *–awl* family with words like *shawl* and *brawl*.

What to Know...

Do you and your kid ever sing "Patty Cake, Patty Cake, Baker's Man"? Your child has probably been listening to rhymes and using word families since he was a baby.

Review these skills with your child this way:

- Words that **rhyme** have the same end sounds, though the endings may be spelled differently, as in *light* and *kite*.

- Words that rhyme may also have the same **spelling pattern** in which the vowel and any following consonants of a syllable are the same, such as *–ight* in *light, fight,* and *right*. (This is also known as having the same **rime**).

- A **word family** is a group of words that rhyme *and* share the same spelling pattern (rime). Word families help kids to write and read new words. New words are created by adding a new sound to the beginning of the spelling pattern.

Read this sentence to your kid:

I might take a bite out of my kite at night.

Ask your child to pick out all of the rhyming words in the sentence. Ask him to pick out the words with the same spelling pattern. Challenge your child to create his own silly rhyming sentences and to draw silly pictures to go along with each sentence.

 *Watch Out!*

Your kid might come up with a rhyme that uses nonsense rhyming words. That's okay! Even though the word may not be a "real" word, your child has shown that she understands rhyming. Just make sure your child knows a nonsense word from an actual word that she can look up in the dictionary.

Review the words shown in the family below.

Talk about why these words are in the same family. Ask your child if he can think of other words that could be part of the *-et* family. Encourage your child to create additional word families (the *-ack* family, *-op* family, *-ike* family). Discuss words that rhyme but have different spelling patterns (rimes) as they come up.

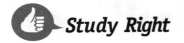 Study Right

Have your child create a word family book using some of the most common first-grade spelling patterns. To make the word family book, write one of the following spelling patterns at the top of each page: *-at, -ot, -ag, -og, -an, -en, -et, -eg, -un, -ip, -ap, -op, -up, -ack, -ock, -ick, -uck, -ing, -ish, -ang, -ash, -ung, -ong, -ink, -ank, -unk.* Ask your kid to list as many words as possible for each word family. She can illustrate the words too. Your child can continue to add new words as her vocabulary grows. This book will become a reference for your child when she wants to spell a word that has the same spelling pattern as a word in this book.

On Your Way to an "A" Activities

{ 10 minutes }

Type: Speaking and Listening
Materials needed: book of nursery rhymes, pencil, paper
Number of players: 2

Choose a poem or a rhyming story from a favorite rhyming book. As you read, stop after rhyming words and ask your child what words she heard that rhyme. Read the poem or story again, this time stopping before reading the second word of a rhyming pair. Ask your child to guess the word before you continue.

{ 15 minutes }

Type: Game/Competitive
Materials needed: pencil, markers or crayons, a set of 20 note cards
Number of players: 2

In this version of "Go Fish," create pairs of rhyming cards with your child by writing each word from a pair on a separate card. Ask your child to illustrate the word. You should have 10 pairs for a total of 20 cards. Each player gets 6 cards. Put the rest of the cards in a pile on the table. Now it's time to try to make rhyming word pairs cards. For example, if your child has the card *cat*, he would ask you, "Do you have a card that rhymes with *cat*?" If you have it, you must give the card to your child. Your child places the pair on the table. If you don't have the card, your child picks one card from the card pile, and then it's your turn. Whoever has the most pairs wins! Here are some suggestions of rhyming pairs that would be easy to illustrate: *cat* and *bat*, *clock* and *rock*, *lips* and *chips*, *bug* and *plug*, *egg* and *leg*, *snake* and *cake*, *feet* and *street*, *night* and *light*, *throat* and *boat*, *king* and *ring*.

First Graders Are...

First graders often benefit from repetition, especially if they're entertained. They actually like to hear the same poem or story again and again, and they'll enjoy the rhyming activity above with several poems.

Has your child breezed through the activities? If so, he or she can work on this Using Your Head activity independently. You'll probably want to read the activity below aloud to your child.

Using Your Head

{20 minutes}

Grab a **pencil**!

Help the trains get to Rhyme Town. Load the trains with the correct rhyming words.

bake cake

book

day

Compound Words

Snowman, raindrop, waterfall, sunflower. Some of the most delightful words in the English language are compound words. Compound words aren't just fun to say. They're also an extremely important tool to help beginning readers.

Since compound words are made up of two smaller words, they are the perfect starting point for kids to get experience with reading longer words. If your child can read the words *snow* and *man* separately, he most likely can read them together! But even if your child can read only *man*, he is already halfway there to reading the complete word. The real trick is to not let these long words intimidate your child.

First things first: Get a sense of what your kid already knows. Turn the page and tell your kid to Jump Right In!

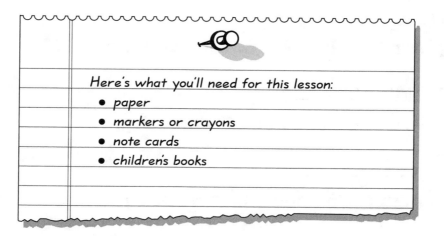

Here's what you'll need for this lesson:

- paper
- markers or crayons
- note cards
- children's books

Feel free to read the questions aloud.

 **Jump Right In!**

Choose the word that completes the compound word.

1. dog_____
   A. puppy   **B.** animal   **C.** cat   **D.** house

2. snow_____
   A. flake   **B.** rain   **C.** star   **D.** flower

3. birth_____
   A. home   **B.** sister   **C.** day   **D.** gift

4. foot_____
   A. step   **B.** shoe   **C.** toe   **D.** leg

5. Jim likes to play foot_____.

    A. line   **B.** ball   **C.** toe

6. I put a letter in the mail_____.

    A. box   **B.** girl   **C.** table

Read the sentence. Circle the compound word and write it on the line.

7. I ate a cupcake for dessert.

_____

8. A rainbow was in the sky yesterday.

_____

9. My bookshelf is full of books.

_____

 **Excellent Job!**

Checking In

A Answers for pages 36 and 37:

1. D

2. A

3. C

4. A

5. B

6. A

7. An A+ answer: cupcake

8. An A+ answer: rainbow

9. An A+ answer: bookshelf

Did your child get the correct answers? If so, make sure she knows what the compound word means. Ask her to use the compound word in a sentence.

Did your child get any of the answers wrong? If so, go over the incorrect answer choices. Check to see that your child didn't just choose a word that relates. For question 4, a shoe goes on a foot, but *footshoe* is not a compound word. For questions 7–9, review each word in the sentence. After you read each word, ask your child to break up the word into two words. If your child cannot do this, the word is not a compound word.

Watch Out!

Your child may invent an "original" compound word. He may even be able to explain to you what it means: "You know, a *snowflower* is when the snow comes down in a shape of a flower." Your creative child has shown that he understands how compound words work. Celebrate his inventiveness by making a book of these made-up compound words. Make sure to explain the difference between "real" compound words and made-up compound words by visiting the dictionary.

What to Know...

Your child knows a lot of words. He or she might not realize that many of those words can be used to make compound words.

Review this skill with your child this way:

- **Compounds words** are words made up of two or more smaller words.

cup   +   cake   =   cupcake

Ask your child to read the word under each picture. Explain to him or her that the two short words come together to make one long word. This kind of long word is called a compound word.

With your kid, fill in the blanks under the pictures below.

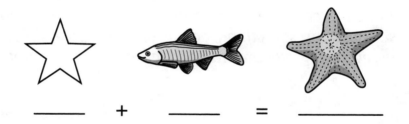

—————   +   —————   =   —————

Ask your child to think about why the words star and fish were used to make the word starfish. Why not use heart and fish? Encourage your child to think of other compound words that contain short words that actually describe the compound word.

Your child can practice using compound words with these activities. You'll probably want to read these activities aloud to your child.

On Your Way to an "A" Activities

{ **20** minutes } Type: Game/Competitive
Materials needed: 20 pieces of paper
Number of players: 2 or more

Play "Snowball Fight! Compound Word Battle." Think of 10 compound words (one can be *snowball*). Write the first part of the word on a blank sheet of paper. Your partner will write the second part of the word on a different blank sheet of paper. Continue until you've used all 10 compound words. Turn each paper into a snowball by crumpling it up. Now you are ready for a snowball battle! Stand on opposite sides of the room and start throwing your snowballs! Once you are done, pick up a snowball. Try to find another snowball that has a word to go with yours to make a compound word. Keep playing until all the matches are found. Here are some compound word suggestions: *something, downstairs, backpack, footprint, birthday, eyebrow, saltwater, railroad, handshake, barefoot.*

{ **20** minutes } Type: Arts and Crafts
Materials needed: paper, markers or crayons
Number of players: independent

Choose a compound word and illustrate it by showing how it is made up of two smaller words. For example, if you choose the compound word *sandbox*, you would draw a picture of sand, then write a + sign, then draw a box, then write an = sign, and finally draw a picture of a sandbox. Show your drawings to someone at home. Can they guess the compound word? Here are some compound word suggestions: *doghouse, flashlight, blackbird, eyeglasses, bedroom.*

First Graders Are...

Drawing is an important outlet for first graders. It can be a way for children to communicate and express themselves, especially since their writing skills are still not fully developed. Don't forget to support your child as he or she continues to doodle.

Type: Active
Materials needed: note cards, pencil
Number of players: 2 or more

Play a game of "Compound Word Charades." Write down several compound words on note cards. Mix up the cards. Players will take turns choosing a card and acting out the word. You can either act out the words by acting out each smaller part, or you can act out the whole word. Try to do a little of each. Any player can guess the word!

Type: Game
Materials needed: 20 note cards, pen, pencil, or markers
Number of players: 2 or more

In this version of "Memory," players will try to pick up pairs of words that will make compound words. Think of 10 compound words. Write the first part of the word on one note card. Write the second part of the word on another note card. Mix up the cards. Lay out all 20 cards facedown on a table. Turn over two cards. If the two cards make a compound word, you get to go again. If it's not a match, return the cards and let another player take a turn. Keep playing until all the matches are found.

 *Study Right*

To continue practicing with compound words, your child can keep a compound word journal to use as he reads books. Have your child write down every new compound word he reads. When your kid sees a compound word again in another book, place a tally mark by the word. Which compound word shows up most often?

Has your child breezed through the activities? If so, he or she can work on this Using Your Head activity independently. You'll probably want to read the activity below aloud to your child.

Using Your Head

[20 minutes]

*Grab some **crayons** or **markers**!*

Help the fish find their matches. If the two fish make a compound word, color them the same color.

Answers: raindrop, homework, sunset, basketball, fingernail

Contructions

Rules, rules, rules! On top of the rules your child has for school, for home, or for playing at a friend's house, she is also learning rules that apply to reading and writing. It's a lot to remember! One particularly tricky rule has to do with contractions. It's easy for kids to get them confused with compound words because they both involve combining two words. With compound words, we take two words and smoosh them together to make a new word. However, with contractions, we take two words and smoosh them together and then replace some letters with an apostrophe. Unlike compound words, the two words that make up a contraction have the same meaning as the contraction.

Your child probably uses contractions all the time when she speaks. The hard part is knowing how to write a contraction and understanding that *do not* has the same meaning as *don't*.

First things first: Get a sense of what your kid already knows. Turn the page and tell your kid to Jump Right In!

Here's what you'll need for this lesson:
- note cards
- paper
- books
- markers or crayons
- glue
- mini elbow macaroni
- pennies

Feel free to read the questions aloud.

 **Jump Right In!**

Choose the correct contraction.

1. is not

    A. she's   **B.** won't   **C.** isn't   **D.** is'nt

2. she is

    A. she'll   **B.** she's   **C.** shes   **D.** he'll

3. you are

    A. you're   **B.** yo'ure   **C.** you'll   **D.** your

4. he would

    A. she'd   **B.** he'd   **C.** they'd   **D.** he's

5. they will

    A. they'll   **B.** they're   **C.** they'd   **D.** he'll

Read the sentences. Find the words that form the underlined contraction.

6. He <u>wasn't</u> in class.

    A. was   **B.** was not   **C.** is not   **D.** will be

7. <u>They're</u> my friends.

    A. you are   **B.** they is   **C.** there are   **D.** they are

Write the two words that form each contraction.

8. didn't   _____   _____

9. won't   _____   _____

Excellent Job!

Checking In

ⓐ Answers for pages 44 and 45:

1. C
2. B
3. A
4. B
5. A
6. B
7. D
8. An A+ answer: did not
9. An A+ answer: will not

Did your child get the correct answers? If so, you could ask, "How did you know where the apostrophe was supposed to go?" You can also ask your child to use the contraction in a sentence to make sure he knows what the contraction means.

Did your child get any of the answers wrong? Take a look at the answers that were chosen. Were they close in spelling? Did she choose the wrong placement of the apostrophe? Make sure your kid gives you an explanation so you know what went wrong. For questions 6 and 7, your child might have chosen an answer choice that also makes sense in the sentence. Remind your child to look for an answer choice that not only makes sense, but also represents the contraction.

Watch Out!

Many contractions sound like other words. Often, first graders will read or write *will* instead of *we'll, your* instead of *you're,* and *were* instead of *we're.* Make sure to point out the different spellings and the apostrophe to get your child to notice the difference between these words. Sometimes your kid might decide not to read a word as a contraction and instead say two words, such as *I am* for *I'm.* Although the two words have the same meaning as the contraction, your child should try to become familiar with reading the contraction correctly. Explain that contractions are a shortened version of the two words.

What to Know...

Your child might regularly use contractions during conversation, but reading and writing contractions may seem like a brand-new concept to her.

Review this skill with your child this way:

- A **contraction** is a word formed by combining two words. Contractions are formed when some of the sounds in the words are replaced by an apostrophe (').

Often, making a contraction means replacing a vowel in the second word with an apostrophe. Review the following steps with your kid to turn *is not* into a contraction.

is not

Step 1:   Take out the vowel in the second word.

is n<s>o</s>t

Step 2:   Replace the vowel with an apostrophe.

is n't

Step 3:   Smoosh all the letters together.

Try the steps together with the following word pairs: *are not, was not, do not, I am.* Remind her how the apostrophe takes the place of the letter or letters you take out.

Sometimes making a contraction is difficult because it's hard to know which letters to replace with an apostrophe. Review these tricky contractions in groups. For example, review the *you'll, he'll, she'll,* and *it'll* together because they all follow the same pattern of replacing the letters *w* and *i* with an apostrophe.

Your child can practice working with contractions using these activities. You'll probably want to read these activities aloud to your child.

On Your Way to an "A" Activities

25 minutes

Type: Arts and Crafts
Materials needed: paper, markers or crayons, glue, mini elbow macaroni
Number of players: independent

Create a contraction poster using elbow macaroni. Use markers to write the contractions on your poster, but glue down a piece of elbow macaroni in place of the apostrophe. Hang your contraction poster somewhere special.

15 minutes

Type: Reading/Writing
Materials needed: a book
Number of players: 2

Choose one of your favorite books. Try reading the book to someone in your family, but instead of reading the book as it's written, try to take out all the contractions and use the two words that make the contraction instead. For example, if a sentence in the book says, *"We're* going to have to work all night," you would read *"We are* going to have to work all night." Challenge someone in your family to do the same when you're finished.

First Graders Are...

Children in first grade love closure. They really need to complete the full activity in order to feel successful. Make sure to give your child specific guidelines on how many pages he should read so he can feel like he's accomplished something. Children need to know exactly what you expect of them.

25 minutes

Type: Game
Materials needed: 4 sheets of paper, 16 note cards, pencil, pennies
Number of players: 2 to 4

Get ready to play "Contraction Bingo." First, ask someone to write down contraction word pairs on each of the 16 note cards. For example, one note card has "is not." Next, ask someone to help you and the other players make bingo cards by drawing a 4 x 4 grid on a piece of paper. Read the words on a note card. Write down the contraction for those words in one of the spaces on your bingo board. You can pick whichever space you want! Continue until you've used all of the note cards. Your bingo card should be complete, and now you're ready to play "Contraction Bingo." Choose one player to call out the word pairs on the note cards. Each player should then find the matching contraction on his or her bingo card and place a penny on that spot. The first player with four markers across, down, or on a diagonal shouts "Bingo!" and wins.

Study Right

Help your child create flash cards with the contraction on one side and the word pairs that make the contraction on the other side. Your kid can study contractions independently using these flash cards.

Has your child breezed through the activities? If so, he or she can work on this Using Your Head activity independently. You'll probably want to read the activity below aloud to your child.

Grab a **pencil** or **pen** and **some crayons**!

Match the mail to the correct mailbox.

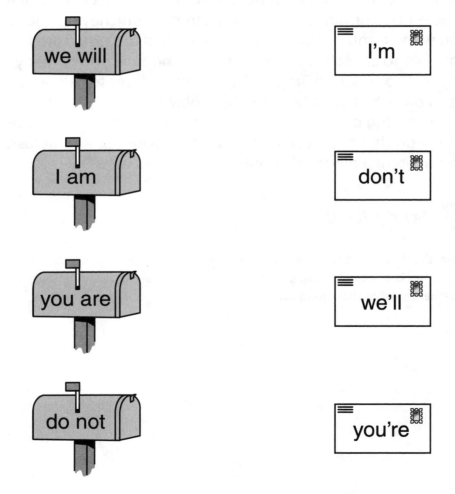

Answers: we will—we'll; I am—I'm; you are—you're; do not—don't

Prefixes and Suffixes

First graders' vocabularies grow pretty fast. This is partly because they're reading a whole lot more than they did in kindergarten, but they're also learning a bit more about the English language. Your child can also use the words she already knows, and add a prefix or a suffix to them to expand her vocabulary. Learning just the most common prefixes (*re–, un–, pre–,* and *mis–*) can help your child learn the meaning of quite a lot of words. Suffixes can be a bit trickier for your child because he might have a hard time figuring out which part of the word is the suffix. Also, their meanings are a little more complicated. Once your child becomes pretty familiar with prefixes and suffixes, however, big words aren't as scary anymore—he will be able to break those words down.

First things first: Get a sense of what your kid already knows. Turn the page and tell your kid to Jump Right In!

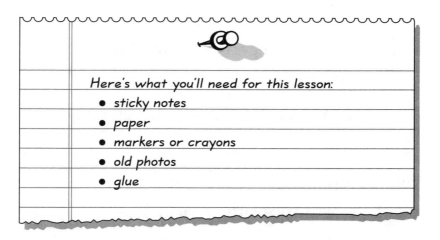

Here's what you'll need for this lesson:
- sticky notes
- paper
- markers or crayons
- old photos
- glue

Jump Right In!

Choose the correct word to complete the sentence.

1. Joe had to _____ the blanket.

   (fold again)

   A. unfold   **B.** prefold   **C.** refold

2. I am _____ because it is raining.

   (not happy)

   A. unhappy   **B.** mishappy   **C.** rehappy

3. My mom has to _____ the door.

   (opposite of lock)

   A. relock   **B.** unlock   **C.** prelock

Choose the word that best matches the definition.

4. more than one car

    A. cars   **B.** uncar   **C.** carful

5. the most strong

    A. strongest   **B.** unstrong   **C.** strongs

Add a prefix or suffix to the base word to make a word that matches the definition.

6. jump

    To jump in the past: _____

7. make

    To make again: _____

Excellent Job!

Checking In

Ⓐ Answers for pages 52 and 53:

1. C
2. A
3. B
4. A
5. A
6. An A+ answer: jumped
7. An A+ answer: remake

Did your child get the correct answers? If so, make sure she understands which part of the word is the base and which part is the prefix or suffix. Check to see if your child understands the meaning of some of the other answer choices. Be sure to skip the made-up words.

Did your child get any of the answers wrong? If so, review the meaning of each prefix and suffix and then ask your child to try answering the questions again. Sometimes a word might make sense in the sentence completions for questions 1 through 3, but does not match the specified definition.

Watch Out!

The suffix –ed is a tricky one. When working with the suffix –ed, help your child understand that the suffix –ed can make three different sounds. It can make the /t/ sound as in *jumped,* the /d/ sound as in *played,* and the /ed/ sound as in *wanted.* When reading with your child, help him sort this out by saying things like, "That *ed* makes the /t/ sound" or "That *ed* makes the /d/ sound." Unfortunately, there's no real rule that explains which sound the *ed* will make. Your child will begin to remember by repeated exposure to reading and listening to words that end in *ed.*

What to Know...

Learning just a few prefixes and suffixes will quickly expand your child's vocabulary.

Review these skills with your child this way:

- A **base word** is a word that can be used to make new words. These words might be seen by themselves or as part of larger words.
- A **prefix** can be added to the beginning of a base word to change its meaning.
- A **suffix** can be added to the end of a base word to change its meaning.

Prefixes and base words fit together like puzzle pieces to make brand-new words. Prefixes change the meanings of words.

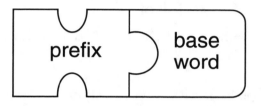

Review the following prefixes and their meanings with your child.

$$un-\ =\ \text{not (or the opposite of)}$$
$$re-\ =\ \text{again}$$
$$pre-\ =\ \text{before}$$
$$mis-\ =\ \text{wrongly}$$

Look at the puzzle pieces below with your child. Check out how the prefix changes the meaning of the base word *happy*.

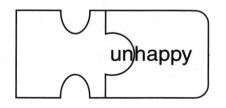

Ask your child the meaning of *unhappy*. Ask your child how the prefix *un-* changed the meaning of the word *happy*. Encourage your child to think of other words that use prefixes.

Suffixes and base words also fit together like puzzle pieces to make brand-new words. Suffixes are at the end of words.

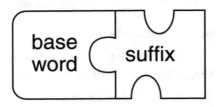

Review the following suffixes and their meanings with your child.

−s = more than one
−ed = happened in the past
−ful = full of
−er = a little more, a little less
−est = most

Look at the puzzle pieces below with your child. Check out how the suffix changes the meaning of the base word *small*.

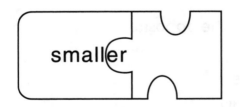

Ask your child the meaning of *smaller*. Ask your child how the suffix −er changed the meaning of the word *small*. Encourage your child to think of other words that use the suffix −er.

 **Watch Out!**

When working with prefixes and suffixes, children tend to misapply the skill. For example, they might read the word *uncle* and identify the *un* as a prefix. When this happens, explain to your kid that sometimes what looks like a prefix or suffix is really just a group of letters. For example, when the letters *un* are removed from *uncle,* no familiar base word is left.

On Your Way to an "A" Activities

Type: Arts and Crafts
Materials needed: old photos, markers or crayons, pencil, paper, glue
Number of players: 2

Create a family album using old photos or drawings of people in your family. Glue down photos or draw a picture of one member of your family on each page. Then, write a sentence that uses a prefix or suffix to describe that person. For example, "My sister is beaut<u>iful</u>." You can also describe someone by comparing him or her to someone else in your family. For example, "My dad is tall<u>er</u> than me." Underline the suffix or prefix you use.

Type: Active
Materials needed: sticky notes, pencil
Number of players: 2

This activity is called "Cool Comparisons." Use a base word and the suffixes –*er* and –*est* to compare things. Look at groups of three similar objects around the house (three books, three people, three chairs, etc.). Describe the objects using comparing words. Write down a comparing word on a sticky note, and stick it on the object. Examples: *big, bigger, biggest*; *small, smaller, smallest*; *soft, softer, softest*; *wide, wider, widest*.

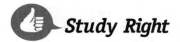 **Study Right**

To help your kid get better at identifying base words, prefixes, and suffixes, have her underline parts of words in different colors. For example, underline base words in red, prefixes in blue, and suffixes in green.

Has your child breezed through the activities? If so, he or she can work on this Using Your Head activity independently. You'll probably want to read the activity below aloud to your child.

Using Your Head

[20 minutes]

*Grab a **pencil**!*

Help build a wall by writing in the correct prefixes and suffixes. Choose a brick from the box.

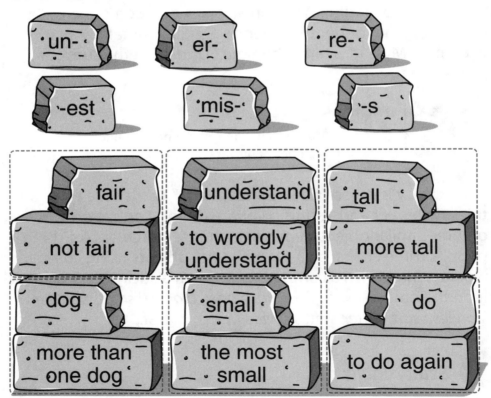

· un- ·   · er- ·   · re- ·

· -est ·   · mis- ·   · -s ·

· fair ·	understand	· tall ·
· not fair ·	· to wrongly understand	more tall
· dog ·	· small ·	· do ·
· more than one dog ·	· the most small	to do again

Before Reading

Much of your child's time in school is spent learning how to read. She spent a lot of time learning how to identify letter sounds in order to put those sounds together to make words. Those skills are very practical, but there is much more to reading. Hopefully, your child has also learned to read for meaning—to understand a good story or learn about a favorite animal.

Think about all the things you and your child have read together. You might have helped your child read stop signs to know how to safely cross the street. You and your child may have read directions to a game. Or perhaps you both read a book about pets to learn about the responsibility of owning a dog. Your child reads for a variety of purposes but may not realize that. If your child has a purpose for reading, he will have a focus, and therefore the reading will be more meaningful. It's important for your child to set his own purpose before reading to create a better interaction between him and the book. Sometimes setting a purpose will be easy for your kid because the title or book cover might have to do with something he already knows about. But sometimes kids have to use clues from the title or cover to set a purpose. If you see your kid struggling with starting a book, ask him to come up with a reason to read the book. This will help make his reading experience more meaningful!

First things first: Get a sense of what your kid already knows. Turn the page and tell your kid to Jump Right In!

Here's what you'll need for this lesson:
- *markers or crayons*
- *note cards*
- *magazines*
- *paper*

Feel free to read the questions aloud.

Jump Right In!

1. Why might you want to read this book?

    A. to learn about animals

    B. to learn about dinosaurs

    C. to laugh about dinosaurs

2. What do you think you'll find out if you read this book?

    A. what dinosaurs ate

    B. how to train your dog

    C. how to bake a cake

3. What would not be in this book?

    A. where dinosaurs lived

    B. how dinosaurs moved

    C. how to use a computer

4. Do you think you would read this book to learn how to do something or to have fun? Why?

5. What do you think this book might be about?

Excellent Job!

Checking In

🅐 Answers for pages 60 and 61:

1. B
2. A
3. C
4. An A+ answer: "I think I would read *Tyler's Adventure in Space* for fun."
5. An A+ answer: "I think this book might be about a boy named Tyler who gets to go on a fun trip in space."

Did your child get the correct answers? If so, help your kid go further into the book by asking him what he already knows about dinosaurs. If he knows quite a bit about dinosaurs, that probably helped him answer the questions.

Did your child get any of the answers wrong? If so, look at the answers your kid chose. Ask her what information she used to choose her answer. Your child might not know how to use clues like the title or the picture on the cover. For questions 4 and 5, point out the picture of the spaceship and the alien.

Watch Out!

Sometimes children often say what they would *like* the story to be about instead of using clues to gain insight into what the story *could* be about. First graders have great imaginations and may need to be reminded to focus on the clues that help make predictions. Remind your child that there is a time and place for a creative mind.

What to Know...

Setting a purpose for reading and making predictions both help your child get ready to read.

Review these skills with your child this way:

- Strong readers often set a **purpose** for reading—they know if they are reading to get information or to have fun.
- **Prior knowledge** is any relevant information we have before we begin reading.
- A **prediction** is an idea or thought about the future.

Ask your kid what each book will be about and why she would want to read the book. Also ask your child what she already knows about each topic or how or she relates to each topic.

Kids should come up with the following purposes for reading each book:

- to learn how to bake a cake
- to get information about airplanes
- to have fun reading a story about Heather's bad day

 *Checking In*

Can your child make accurate predictions about each book? Your first grader might not think to use information she already has to help make predictions. To access your child's prior knowledge, ask specific questions like, "What does this picture (or title) remind you of?" or "What do you already know about this topic?"

Your child can practice before-reading skills with these activities. You'll probably want to read these activities aloud to your child.

On Your Way to an "A" Activities

{ **30** minutes }
Type: Arts and Crafts
Materials needed: 2 sheets paper, markers or crayons
Number of players: 2

Book covers can tell us a lot about a book just from the picture and title. Imagine you're a famous artist who's been asked to create two different book covers. One of these should be for a book someone would want to read for fun. The other cover should be for a book someone would read to get information about something. It's up to you to create the title and all the artwork for the cover. When you're finished, show your work to another person and have them make predictions about the books.

First Graders Are...

First graders are very shy about taking risks. The task of drawing pictures like a famous illustrator may seem daunting. Encourage your child to do his best and praise his creations, even if they're just stick figures and doodles.

{ **15** minutes }
Type: Game/Competitive
Materials needed: note cards
Number of players: 2 or more

Before reading a book, good readers try to think of everything they already know about the topic to make the book easier to read. For this game, you will practice searching your mind for information you already know. Take six note cards. On three of them, write the name of three different people you and the other player know. On the other three, write the name of three animals. Exchange cards with another player. Each player should write five things he or she already knows about each person or animal. It can be anything: favorite food, age, or even hair color.

20 minutes

Type: Active
Materials needed: 5 sheets of paper, pencil
Number of players: 2

For this activity, you're going on a book, magazine, or newspaper hunt. Hunt around your house to find five books, magazines, or newspapers that you would read to get information and five that you would read for fun. Then, think of at least one thing you already know about the topic for each. For the fun books, magazines, or newspapers, make at least one prediction of what you think might happen.

20 minutes

Type: Speaking/Listening
Materials needed: magazines
Number of players: 2

Pictures are some of the best clues to use when trying to make a prediction about a text. Take a look at your favorite magazines. Each player should pick a picture that is interesting to him or her. Take turns making up stories about your picture. Give the people names. Tell what they're doing and what they'll do next. Make sure there's something in the picture to support your prediction.

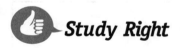 *Study Right*

To give your child a little extra practice with making predictions, use his favorite TV show or movie. During commercial breaks (or when you press pause), ask your kid what he thinks will happen next. Get him to support each prediction with details from the show or movie.

Has your child breezed through the activities? If so, he or she can work on this Using Your Head activity independently. You'll probably want to read the activity below aloud to your child.

Using Your Head

Grab a **pencil**!

Read page 2 of *Tyler's Adventure in Space.*

The spaceship landed. Tyler could hear voices from inside.

Using predictions and what you know about aliens, write and illustrate page 3.

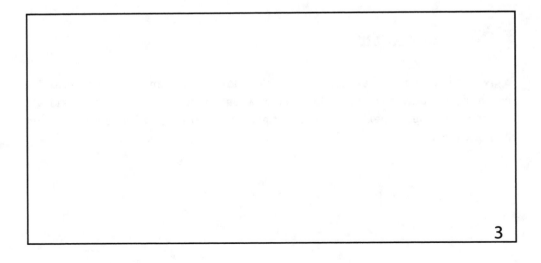

3

During Reading: Making Connections

Reading opens up doors to the world. Your child can venture into new worlds from the comfort of the couch. For these experiences to come alive, it helps if your kid can make some kind of connection to what is happening in the book. Has your child visited a zoo similar to the zoo in the book? Does the main character have similar qualities to your child's best friend? Has your child experienced a problem similar to the one in the book? Does the book remind your child of another book? The more your child can relate to a book, the better he will understand the book and enjoy it!

First graders need to be taught how to make connections while they are reading. This means that your kid shouldn't just read the story quickly without stopping. Try to remind your child that it's not a race. Encourage her to pause from time to time to try to connect with something in the story. Even though your child is only six or seven years old, she most likely has had a wealth of experiences so far that will lead to several connections.

First things first: Get a sense of what your kid already knows. Turn the page and tell your kid to Jump Right In!

Here's what you'll need for this lesson:
- *paper*
- *markers or crayons*
- *notecards*

Jump Right In!

Read the poem and the story below and answer the questions that follow.

The Falling Ball

The ball is flying over the wall.
Oh no! I think it's going to fall.
I could try to catch it,
But I'm so very small.
I think I'll call my friend the giant.
He's 24 feet tall.
He'll climb the wall and catch the ball
And throw it back to me.
That's all.

Alan's First School Friend

Alan could not fall asleep. Tomorrow was his first day of first grade and he was scared. He didn't know anyone at school. In the morning, he got up, got dressed, and walked to school. When Alan got to his class, he saw one desk left next to a giant. This made Alan even more scared. Alan looked over at the giant. The giant gave Alan a nice, big smile. Maybe he would be Alan's first school friend!

1. What do the poem and the story have in common?

   A. They both have characters named Alan.

   B. They both are about first grade.

   C. They both have giants.

2. Which part of the story could <u>not</u> happen in real life?

   A. A boy could be in first grade.

   B. A boy could have trouble sleeping.

   C. A boy could have a giant in his classroom.

3. What did the story "Alan's First School Friend" remind you of?

Excellent Job!

Checking In

ⓐAnswers for page 69:

1. C
2. C
3. An A+ answer: "It reminded me of the time I was scared for the first day of school."

Did your child get the correct answers? If so, have her give you details that support each answer. For question 1, ask your child to find the place in both texts that mentions a giant.

Did your child get any of the answers wrong? If so, ask him to explain his rationale. For example, if your child answered B for question 2, perhaps he has never had trouble sleeping, and therefore it's difficult to make a connection.

Watch Out!

Sometimes kids have trouble making connections to texts because they think that their connection has to involve all of the same details. For example, in question 3, your child might tell you that she has never met a giant. Explain to your child that she does not have to connect to the entire story; a connection to just a piece of this story is great! If your child is still having difficulty, help by asking specific questions like, "Have you ever been scared?" or "Do you remember your first school friend?"

What to Know...

Making connections is similar to playing "Connect the Dots": the more lines your kid can draw between the text and himself, the world, and other texts, the clearer the picture becomes.

Review these skills with your child this way:

- **Text-to-self connections** are when you build links and relationships between the text and your everyday life, personal experiences, and private thoughts or feelings.

- **Text-to-world connections** are when you build links and relationships between the text and the world. You can link details from the text with things you see in the world and events going on in the world.

- **Text-to-text connections** are when you build links and relationships between texts or different parts of a text. You can link details from the beginning of a text to the end of a text. You can also build links and relationships between different texts and link details between them, such as from a poem to a story or from a story to another story.

Your child can practice making different types of connections using the following picture.

Ask your child to look at the picture. Ask, "Does anything about the picture remind you of the poem "'The Falling Ball'?" Ask, "Does it remind you of anything that happened to you?" Ask, "Does it remind you about another person you know?"

Ask your child to make connections as he or she reads the following story.

The New Baby

Paula was getting a new sister. She was at home with her grandma waiting for her mom and dad to get back from the hospital with her new baby sister. Paula was scared. She did not know what to do with a baby, and she was scared the baby would not like her.

She heard the door open. She went to the door and saw her mom walk in with her new sister, Lauren, wrapped in a blanket. As soon as she saw the cute baby, she was not scared anymore.

Here are some examples of **text-to-self** connections:

- I met my baby cousin when she came home from the hospital.
- My grandma watches me when my mom and dad go out.

Here is an example of a **text-to-text** connection:

- I read another book about a new baby coming home, and the sister was very jealous.

Here is an example of a **text-to-world** connection:

- I know babies can cry a lot, but it doesn't mean that they don't like someone.

 *Checking In*

Is your child having trouble making text-to-text and text-to-world connections? With text-to-text connections, children often have difficulty keeping the details of each text clear in their minds. It can be helpful to ask your child specific questions to jog his memory, such as, "Have you read another book that is about a new baby?" With text-to-world connections, children might have difficulty because their sense of the world is so abstract. Remind your child of familiar things in his world, such as a relative or someone from the neighborhood who has a new baby.

Your child can practice making connections with these activities. You'll probably want to read these activities aloud to your child.

On Your Way to an "A" Activities

{ **15** minutes }

Type: Arts and Crafts
Materials needed: 1 large sheet of paper, markers or crayons
Number of players: independent

You probably have connections with a lot of people! Choose 10 people you know. Draw a picture of each person around the border of your paper. Then, draw yourself in the middle. Underneath each person, write a sentence telling one way you connect with that person. Do you both have the same favorite food? Do you both have the same color hair? Draw a line to connect you to each person.

{ **20** minutes }

Type: Active
Materials needed: none
Number of players: 2

To play "That Reminds Me of…," walk around the house with your partner. Look for objects that remind you of other times or places. For example, you might see an apple in the kitchen and say, "That reminds me of the time I went apple picking." Or you might see a candle and say, "That reminds me of the time we lost power and had to use candles." Challenge your partner to think of a connection to the same object.

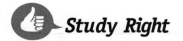 *Study Right*

If your child needs extra practice with making connections, create note cards with the following questions written on them: What does this remind me of in my life? Has something like this ever happened to me? What were my feelings when I read this? What does this remind me of in another book I've read? How is this book similar to things that happen in the real world? Your child can use these cards as he or she reads.

Using Your Head

{ **20** minutes }

*Grab a **pencil**!*

Read the passage about chimpanzees. Then, make connections.

Young chimpanzees learn a lot from watching their mothers. They watch to learn which food is safe to eat and where ripe food can be found. For the first few months of its life, a baby chimp hangs on to the hair of its mother's belly wherever she travels.

Text-to-Self: _____

_____

Text-to-World: _____

_____

Text-to-Text: _____

_____

During Reading: Checking Understanding

When your child is reading a story, how do you really know whether he understands what is going on in the story? Of course you can ask your child questions, but you're not always going to be there every single time your child picks up a book. Your kid is growing up and starting to learn how to become a more mature reader. One skill your child is learning is how to assess whether or not he understands what he has read.

Young readers, especially, need help training themselves to be aware of when they are or are not understanding a story. Sometimes they're working so hard to sound out words that the meaning is lost completely, and they don't even realize it. You can teach your child to stop regularly and try to picture the story in her mind. If your kid is having difficulty with that, she might need to back up and reread a section. You can also teach your child to ask herself questions. If the question somehow relates to the story, you know that your kid is following the story and is naturally curious. Your child will learn that it's best to try to catch something confusing early on rather than get to the end of a book and feel completely lost.

First things first: Get a sense of what your kid already knows. Turn the page and tell your kid to Jump Right In!

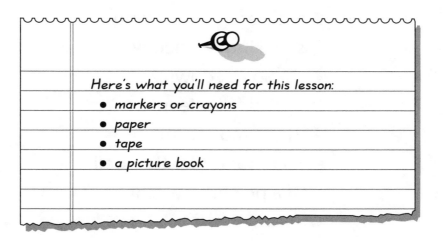

Here's what you'll need for this lesson:
- *markers or crayons*
- *paper*
- *tape*
- *a picture book*

 **Jump Right In!**

Read the poem and answer the questions that follow.

The Witch

She stands in her kitchen
Boiling and bubbling,
Toiling and troubling.
As I watch her
I feel itchy and twitchy,
Crawly and creepy.
Whatever she is cooking
Is making me sleepy.
So I sit down
And fall asleep.
I don't move a stitch.
I've been put under the spell
Of a powerful witch!

1. Where do you think the witch might live?

A.   **B.**   **C.**

2. What might the character's face look like as he or she is staring at the witch?

A.   **B.**   **C.**

3. What do you want to know about the witch?

4. What do you want to know about the character watching the witch?

Excellent Job!

 *Checking In*

Answers for page 77:

1. B
2. A
3. An A+ answer: "I want to know if she put some magic in whatever she is cooking."
4. An A+ answer: "I want to know why the character stays there watching the witch if he or she feels itchy and twitchy."

Did your child get the correct answers? If so, find out how your child chose each answer. For example, for question 1 ask, "How did you know a witch's house would look like that?" Your child might have read another story about a witch or realized that gardens and schools aren't places that people live.

Did your child get any of the answers wrong? Ask your child to explain his reasoning by using text from the poem. You can also encourage your child to pretend to be the character in the poem. Ask, "What face would you make if you were feeling itchy and twitchy?"

 *Watch Out!*

Some topics get first graders so excited that they actually go off topic. For example, your child might have tons of questions about witches like, "How do they ride through the sky on a broom?" and "Why do most witches have big warts on their noses?" Point out that question 3 is actually referring to a specific witch: the witch in the poem. Encourage your child to think of questions that relate to the witch in the poem.

What to Know...

Checking for understanding is a natural part of the reading process.

Review these skills with your child this way:

- Strong readers develop their comprehension by **picturing the story,** or imagining the details and the actions as they read.

- Strong readers are curious and **ask questions** as they read. They ask questions about the details, they wonder about the story, and they are curious about what they are reading.

Questions can often come from the illustrations. These questions can lead to visualizations.

Talk with your child about the illustration. Ask your child what might be behind the door. Ask your child to describe the picture in his or her head.

 *Checking In*

Do your child's visualizations make sense? If so, ask your kid to then visualize the actions of the characters. What might the mom say to her daughter? What would the daughter say back? If your kid is having trouble visualizing, discuss the details in the illustration. Talking about the illustration and noticing details may help lead your child to visualizations and questions.

Your child can practice picturing the story, asking questions, and making predictions using the following story.

> Kayla did not want to go to the dentist's office. Today she had to get an X-ray. She was crying and holding her mom. The last time she went to the dentist's office, she did not have a good time. It was terrible!
>
> She had to sit in a big, scary chair. She had to open her mouth for a long time. It was like brushing her teeth for an hour. It felt like she had sand in her mouth. Kayla did not want to think about what might happen in the X-ray room.

Ask your child to think of questions and predictions based on the story.

Here are some examples of questions:

- Why does Kayla have to get an X-ray?
- Why did it feel like sand was in her mouth?

Here is an example of a prediction:

- I think the dentist might be extra nice to Kayla this time because he knows she had a terrible time at her last visit.

 *Checking In*

Is your child having a hard time thinking of good questions? If so, role-play with your kid. Pretend to be Kayla, acting scared. Your child can pretend to be Kayla's mother. What might the mother ask Kayla? Sometimes, all your child needs is a little dramatization to get going. Remember to make sure your child tries to answer his questions!

Your child can practice visualizing, asking questions, and making predictions with these activities. You'll probably want to read these activities aloud to your child.

On Your Way to an "A" Activities

15 minutes

Type: Game/Competitive
Materials needed: none
Number of players: 2

Play "20 Questions" with a partner. Think of a person whom you and your partner both know, but don't tell your partner who it is. Get a good picture of that person in your mind. Your partner can ask you up to 20 questions to help him or her guess who you're thinking of. The questions can have only yes or no answers. If your partner guesses the person, he or she gets a point. Then it's your partner's turn to think of someone and your turn to ask the questions. Whoever gets the most points wins!

30 minutes

Type: Arts and Crafts
Materials needed: a picture book, white paper, tape, markers or crayons
Number of players: independent

Choose a picture book you haven't read and cover up all of the pictures with white paper. Begin to read the book. As you read each page, draw a new picture to show what you're picturing in your head. When you finish, you'll have a brand-new book!

20 minutes

Type: Speaking/Listening
Materials needed: paper and pencil
Number of players: 2

Pretend you are a news reporter. Pick someone in your house to interview. Have this person tell you a story about an important event in his or her life. Then, ask at least five questions having to do with the story. When you're done, switch roles!

Using Your Head

{ **20** minutes }

*Grab a **pencil**!*

Look at the picture below and answer the questions.

"Well, I guess my day can't get any worse," said Derek.

1. What's a good question you could ask to help you understand the picture?

   A. Who is Derek's teacher?

   B. Where does Derek go to school?

   C. How did Derek's tray fall?

2. What do you think Derek's mom might say when she picks him up from school? Tell someone at home your answer.

Answer: 1. C; 2. She might tell Derek to take a shower.

Cracking the First Grade

During Reading: Expression

Your child might like to hear his favorite story over and over again. Perhaps he loves a certain character in that story or gets excited to reach the happy ending. But how you read the story also makes a difference in your child's enjoyment. Do you change your voice when a character is talking? Do you read with feeling during sad parts and happy parts? Do your facial expressions change during a scary part?

Expression and intonation can make a world of difference when reading a story. Without them, a story is rather dull and lifeless. Punctuation marks bring life to a story by helping kids figure out how to read with expression. Think about the difference between these two sentences:

"Hand me that pencil, please."

"Hand me that pencil, please!"

A simple exclamation point turns a pleasant request into a sharp demand.

Expression is a powerful comprehension strategy. Once your child begins reading with expression, not only will reading become more enjoyable, but she also will better understand what was read.

First things first: Get a sense of what your kid already knows. Turn the page and tell your kid to Jump Right In!

Here's what you'll need for this lesson:
- *household objects*
- *paper*

Feel free to read the questions aloud.

 **Jump Right In!**

Read the sentences. Choose the correct end mark for each sentence.

1. We are going to the park _____

    A. .   **B.** ?   **C.** !

2. When are we going to the park _____

    A. .   **B.** ?   **C.** !

3. Stop picking on me _____

    A. .   **B.** ?   **C.** !

4. I've never seen anything so great in my whole life _____

    A. .   **B.** ?   **C.** !

5. What did you do yesterday _____

    A. .   **B.** ?   **C.** !

6. My favorite color is blue _____

    A. .   **B.** ?   **C.** !

7. Write a sentence that ends with a question mark (?).

8. Write a sentence that ends with an exclamation point (!).

Excellent Job!

 *Checking In*

❹Answers for pages 84 and 85:

1. A
2. B
3. C
4. C
5. B
6. A
7. An A+ answer: "What time is it?"
8. An A+ answer: "That movie was amazing!"

Did your child get the correct answers? If so, check to see if your child can read each sentence with proper expression and intonation.

Did your child get any of the answers wrong? If so, ask your child to read each sentence with the chosen punctuation. If your child is unable to identify the sentences that ask questions or show excitement, review the uses of exclamation points and question marks. If your child reads each sentence using a flat tone, he or she might have difficulty reading without punctuation, and therefore reads the sentence as if it ends with a period. Try reading each sentence to your child using a period, then a question mark, and finally an exclamation point. Ask your child which sentence sounds best. Continue this process until your child feels more comfortable with the different types of punctuation.

 *Watch Out!*

Questions 3 and 4 might be tricky because different kids get excited or show emotion over different things. Your child might think that seeing something great deserves only a period—it's just not that exciting. Have your kid read the sentence both ways—with a period and with an exclamation point—and then decide which one sounds better.

What to Know...

Reading can be boring if your child doesn't use expression.

Review this skill with your child this way:

- Reading with **expression** means reading with a particular tone of voice and using facial features to show feeling.

Periods, question marks, and exclamation points can help you read with expression.

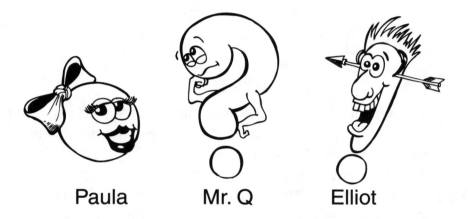

Paula   Mr. Q   Elliot

Look at the pictures of the three end marks with your kid. Tell the story of each mark:

Paula the Polite Period is very well mannered. She never raises her voice, asks questions, or gets too excited. She tells you only things you need to know.

Mr. Q the Curious Question Mark is very, very nosy. He only asks questions and that's it. Everything he says usually starts with words like *who, what, where, when, why, how, can,* and *do*. At the end of every sentence, his voice goes up so that you know he's asking a question.

Elliot the Emotional Exclamation Point is so excited! He's always letting his feelings show—whether he's excited, shocked, or angry, he always has feeling in his voice.

Have your child practice reading the following sentences using expression.

1. Don't touch my toys!
2. A penguin cannot fly.
3. Where are we going tonight?

Ask your child to read the following story with feeling, paying attention to the punctuation marks.

Dinner Time

It is time for dinner. I go downstairs to see what my dad is cooking. No one is in the kitchen. Wait! I see my mom walking into the kitchen with a box. Yay! We are having pizza! What kind of pizza are we having? I will take a look. It's cheese and pepperoni. I'll grab myself a slice. Ouch! It's hot! "Dad, do we have soda to go with our pizza? I want orange soda please." Oh, I'm stuffed!

Watch Out!

Some kids forget to pause after a period. Model pausing for periods for your child by rereading the first three sentences in the story.

Checking In

Was your child able to read the story using proper expression and intonation? If so, show your child the following technique for expressive reading. Choose an important word in each sentence and call attention to it by saying it a bit louder or by stretching if out to make it last a bit longer. Try it with the word *soda* in this sentence: "Dad, do we have soda to go with our pizza?" If your child is having trouble reading with expression, ask your child to read the story again, this time much more slowly. This will help your child pay closer attention to the punctuation marks. You can also model an expressive reading of the story for your child. Then, read the story again in a flat tone. Ask your child which reading made more sense.

Your child can practice using expression and punctuation marks with these activities. You'll probably want to read these activities aloud to your child.

On Your Way to an "A" Activities

Type: Game/Competitive
Materials needed: paper, pencils
Number of players: 2

In "Guess the Mark," each person will write down six sentences—two with periods, two with question marks, and two with exclamation points. Take turns reading your sentences out loud to your partner with expression. Based on your expression, your partner has to guess the end mark of your sentence.

Type: Speaking/Listening
Materials needed: paper, pencil, household objects
Number of players: 2 or more

Create a play about the first day of school. There are two characters: a first grader and a teacher. Everyone else in the class is late. Have someone help you write the script. Don't forget to use periods, exclamation points, and question marks. When you are done, look around your house for any needed objects to use as props. Now it's time to perform your play. Make sure each person in the play has a script. Remember, good actors use expression!

First Graders Are...

First graders are incredibly dramatic. Take full advantage of that trait when acting out your play. Encourage your child to shout, scream, and show as much emotion as possible. Your kid will love it!

Has your child breezed through the activities? If so, he or she can work on this Using Your Head activity independently. You'll probably want to read the activity below aloud to your child.

Using Your Head

Grab a **pencil**!

Read each riddle and write the correct punctuation mark in the box.

1. I am very polite. I never ask questions or show emotion. When you see me in a story, you should pause. What am I?
_____

2. I show a lot of emotion. When you see me at the end of the sentence, make sure to read that sentence with a lot of feeling. What am I? _____

3. I come at the end of an asking sentence. When you read a sentence with me at the end, your voice should go up a little at the end to show that you're curious. What am I?
_____

Answers: 1. . 2. ! 3. ?

After Reading

How many times have you tried to tell a story to an uninterested audience and ended up saying, "Well, I guess you just had to be there"? Stories that end like that are usually the fault of the storyteller. Summarizing an event is an art, and if you choose the wrong details to include or if you get too wordy, then you lose your audience.

When summarizing stories that your child has read, your kid needs to be able to pick out the right details and retell the story in his or her own words. The crucial part is making sure the meaning isn't lost. Summarizing is key because it helps the child, parent, and teacher know whether or not the child has gathered the true essence of what was read.

First things first: Get a sense of what your kid already knows. Turn the page and tell your kid to Jump Right In!

Here's what you'll need for this lesson:
- paper
- tape
- markers or crayons
- 5 DVDs
- art supplies
- stapler

 **Jump Right In!**

Read the story and answer the questions that follow.

The Road Trip

Kathleen was moving fast. Her dad was in the car waiting for her. Her brother, David, was telling her to move faster. This was her first big summer trip. She didn't want to forget anything.

She ran downstairs. Her dad and brother were waiting in the car. Her dad honked the horn.

"Let's go!" Kathleen's dad said.

They were on their way to California. Yes. California. Warm weather. Palm trees. Beaches. It all sounded wonderful to Kathleen. Then she remembered that California was three days away. She would be in the car for three days. No friends. No TV. No video games. Just a radio, her loud brother, and her dad, who loved to sing old songs that she'd never heard of.

It was going to be three very long days.

1. Who is the story mostly about?
   A. Kathleen
   B. David
   C. Dad

2. What is the story about?
   A. California's beaches
   B. car radios and singing
   C. going on a family trip

3. Why does Kathleen think the days will be very long?

Excellent Job!

 **Checking In**

A Answers for page 93:

    1. A

    2. C

    3. An A+ answer: "Kathleen thinks the days will be long because she will have nothing to do in the car, and her brother and dad will annoy her."

Did your child get the correct answers? If so, ask your child to extend his or her answer for question 1 by saying one sentence that explains what the story is about.

Did your child get any of the answers wrong? If so, ask your child to keep questions 1 through 3 in mind as you reread the story aloud. This can help your child focus on the story. Sometimes kids think this is cheating because they think they need to remember details from a story the first time it is read. Explain to your child that it is perfectly okay to revisit the story to find an answer to a question.

 **Watch Out!**

Sometimes kids get mixed up between details and what the whole story is about. In question 2, your child might have chosen (A) California's beaches or (B) car radios and singing. Although these are both mentioned in the story, they do not tell what the whole story is about. Encourage your child to think about whether each answer choice is a detail or tells what the whole story is about.

What to Know...

A good summary gives enough information to get anyone excited about a book!

Review these skills with your child this way:

- A **detail** is a small part of a story.
- A **summary** is a retelling of the most important information in a passage or the main points of a story. A summary includes the topic, the major events, and the important characters. A summary is usually short.

Your child can use his or her hand to identify the details of a story.

Ask your child to use his or her hand to remember the details in "The Road Trip." Then, ask your child to use the details to give a summary of the story.

 **Checking In**

Make sure your child knows how to use each finger in the hand to identify details. If your child is stuck, ask questions that begin with each word. For example: **Who** is in the story? **What** happened? **Where** does the story take place? **When** does the story take place? **Why** did _____ happen?

 **Watch Out!**

Summary and *detail* are big vocabulary words for first graders, and they often mix up the two. Help your kid remember which is which by adding the words onto a hand. Write the word *detail* on each finger and the word *summary* in the palm of the hand.

Your child can practice using details and summarizing with these activities. You'll probably want to read these activities aloud to your child.

On Your Way to an "A" Activities

Type: Game/Competitive
Materials needed: none
Number of players: 2 or more

In "Attention to Detail," you and the other players will have to pay close attention to all the aspects of a room in your house. One person will leave the room, and the players still in the room have to change one detail about the room. You may do things like move a trash can, put a pillow on the floor, or open a cupboard door. The player who left has to return and try to notice what was changed. Take turns being the player to leave the room.

Type: Speaking/Listening
Materials needed: none
Number of players: 2 or more

Play "School Newscaster" with your friends. Each of you will pick two events that happened at school this week. Pretend that you're a newscaster on TV reporting the school news. Include only the important details from the event, and try to make your report short but interesting! Take turns reporting.

Type: Reading/Writing
Materials needed: pencil, paper, 5 DVDs that you've seen, tape
Number of players: independent

You get to be a movie critic for a day! Take five DVDs that you've watched. Write a summary of each movie that includes the who, what, where, when, and why. Write it on a piece of paper and tape it to the outside of the DVD. If your friends or someone in your family wants to watch one of these movies, they'll know exactly what each one is about.

Type: Reading/Writing
Materials needed: paper, pencil, markers or crayons, art supplies, stapler
Number of players: independent

It's time to design your very own diary. Ask someone at home to help you staple several pieces of paper together to make a diary. Next, decorate the cover of your diary. Make sure to include your name. Write in your diary once each day. You should write a summary of the day using a lot of details. You can draw a picture to go along with your entry. When you are done, don't forget to put your diary in a special place, and don't forget to write in it the next day!

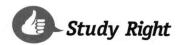

Study Right

For extra practice with summarizing, create a graphic organizer for your child by drawing a large hand on a piece of paper. After your child finishes a story, ask him or her to fill out the details in each finger. Then, ask your child to use the details to write a summary in the palm of the hand.

Using Your Head

{ **15** minutes }

*Grab a **pencil**!*

Look at the picture of Kathleen and her family. Then, answer the questions.

1. What is Kathleen doing?

　　A. singing

　　B. playing a game

　　C. looking bored

2. Which is an important detail?

　　A. the size of the car

　　B. Kathleen frowning

　　C. the color of Kathleen's shirt

Answers: 1. C; 2. B

Using Context Clues

Kids—especially first graders—love to ask questions. You might hear a lot of "Why?" "How?" and "What?" It's great that kids are so curious about the world. However, it is also important to teach kids how to begin to answer those kinds of questions themselves (when possible).

In school, your child is learning to do this through the use of context clues. If your kid comes to a confusing word in a story, he or she has probably been taught to look at the words and sentences around it (the context clues) to help figure out its meaning. This skill will not only help increase your child's vocabulary, but it will also help your child to become a more successful and independent reader.

First things first: Get a sense of what your kid already knows. Turn the page and tell your kid to Jump Right In!

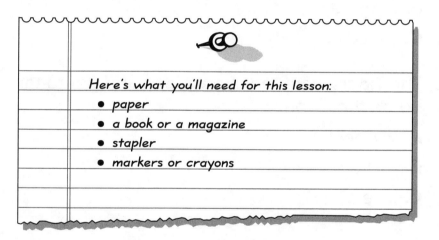

Here's what you'll need for this lesson:
- paper
- a book or a magazine
- stapler
- markers or crayons

Feel free to read the questions aloud.

Jump Right In!

Read each sentence. Choose the answer that best matches the meaning of the words in bold.

1. Emily **hollered** loudly when she fell off her bike.

   A. whispered

   B. jumped

   C. yelled

2. The Tigers were the **champions** and got to take home the trophy.

   A. winners

   B. players

   C. losers

Cracking the First Grade

Choose the word to complete the sentence.

3. My dad needs to wash his _____ because he drove through a mud puddle.

    A. pencil

    B. dishes

    C. car

4. My stomach is full because I _____ so much food.

    A. ate

    B. threw out

    C. jumped over

Read the story and answer the question that follows.

The hamster was in his cage <u>nibbling</u> on food. In the quiet room, you could hear the sounds of the hamster's teeth hitting the tiny seeds.

5. The word *nibbling* means:

Excellent Job!

 *Checking In*

Answers for pages 100 and 101:

1. C
2. A
3. C
4. A
5. An A+ answer: *Nibbling* means the same as *chewing*.

Did your child get the correct answers? If so, ask your child, "Which hints in each sentence helped you figure out your answer?" Check to see if your child understands each bolded word in questions 1 and 2 by asking her to use it in another sentence.

Did your child get any of the answers wrong? If so, ask your child to say each sentence using the incorrect answer choice. Point out how the clues don't match the incorrect answer choice. For example, in question 2, ask your child if a team that loses a tournament gets to take home a trophy. Help your child underline important clues in the sentence, and then ask your child to try again.

 *Watch Out!*

For question 5, your child might be confused by several of the words in the story. It's possible that your child doesn't have much background knowledge about hamsters. If this is the case, ask your child which other words are confusing, and explain all of the words except *nibbling*. Now your child can focus his attention on just one word.

What to Know...

When reading, children not only have to figure out what a word says, but also what a word means. And if they've never heard that word before, the task of understanding the word might be pretty difficult. That's where context clues come in. Your child can use context clues to figure out what new words mean.

Review this skill with your child this way:

- **Context clues** are words or parts of a sentence that help you understand the meaning of an unfamiliar word.

Your child might be used to looking for clues in pictures to help make sense of what is happening in a story.

Ask your child to tell you what is happening in this picture. Ask your child which clues in the picture helped him or her know.

Most kids will be able to tell you that the picture shows a boy watching a baseball fly into a window of someone's house. The boy might have been the person who hit the ball into the window. Your child might have used the following clues:

- The boy is wearing a baseball jersey and baseball hat.
- The boy is holding a bat and standing on a baseball field.
- The boy has a surprised look on his face.
- The picture shows that the ball came from the baseball field.
- The window looks broken.

Picture clues don't always help your child with comprehension. When a sentence is confusing because of an unfamiliar word, your child can use context clues.

Ask your child to use context clues to figure out the meaning of the words in bold.

Brad and Ian wouldn't stop talking in class. Their **chattering** was making the teacher very upset.

Checking In

Was your child able to use the context clues to figure out the meaning of *chattering*? If not, point out surrounding words and phrases such as *talking* and *making the teacher upset*. Ask your child, "Why do you think the teacher was upset?"

Tomorrow we are going on vacation to Hawaii. I made sure to pack everyone's swimsuit and sunblock in our **luggage.**

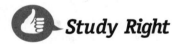

Checking In

Can your child tell you the meaning of *luggage*? If so, which context clues did your child use? If not, point out the words *vacation* and *pack* in the sentences. Ask your child, "Where do you pack your things for vacation?"

Study Right

When your child comes to an unfamiliar word, it might be helpful to underline that word in one color—for example, red. Then, ask your child to look for clues in that sentence or in the sentences nearby. Underline those clues in another color—for example, blue. This can help your child focus on the clue words to help find meaning in the unfamiliar word.

Your child can practice using context clues with these activities. You'll probably want to read these activities aloud to your child.

On Your Way to an "A" Activities

20 minutes

Type: Speaking/Listening
Materials needed: none
Number of players: 2

For this activity, you get to create new words! Make up a word and decide what it means. Make sure it's a word that doesn't exist, like *pleeps* or *chep*. Next, say a sentence with the new word. Your partner has to guess what the word means. Make sure there are enough context clues in each sentence so that your partner will be able to guess what the word means. For example, "I use my *pleeps* to catch balls at baseball practice." If your partner guesses correctly, it is his or her turn to give you a sentence with a new word.

20 minutes

Type: Speaking/Listening
Materials needed: favorite book or a magazine
Number of players: 2

In this activity, players will take turns choosing sentences from a book or kid's magazine. Read a few sentences aloud, leaving out one important word. Your partner will have to use the context clues to guess the missing word. If your partner needs more help, show him or her the matching picture if there is one. Once your partner guesses correctly, it is his or her turn to read a sentence aloud.

👍 Study Right

The more your child reads, the more your child will come into contact with new vocabulary words. Help your child keep track of these new vocabulary words by showing him how to make a dictionary. Staple 13 pages together so that each side is for a letter of the alphabet. Write a letter of the alphabet at the top of each page. Your child can add the new words and definitions to this dictionary as he reads. It will be helpful to also include a picture. Your child can reference this dictionary whenever he reads, especially if the context clues for a particular word aren't helpful. (Your kid could use the alphabet book he made on page 26 to keep track of new vocabulary words.)

Using Your Head

{15 minutes}

Grab a **pencil**!

Read the story. Match each word with its correct meaning.

Julia came home from school. "I'm going to bed!" she **exclaimed** to her mother, who was in the other room. Julia walked up to her room. She let out a big yawn. Her eyes were closing as she walked to her bed. She was so **familiar** with her room that she knew when she had to step over something or walk around something. She got into bed and said, "I'm **tuckered out**!" In less than five seconds, Julia was fast asleep!

1. exclaimed   **A.** tired

2. familiar   **B.** shouted

3. tuckered out   **C.** know really well

Answers: 1. B; 2. C; 3. A

Drawing Conclusions

If your child sees a person yawning, she can probably figure out that the person is tired. If your child sees a person shivering and reaching for a jacket, she can probably guess that the person is cold. Your child notices little details like this every day. These details help your kid draw conclusions about someone or something.

In school, your child is learning to draw conclusions while reading and listening to books. In first grade, the stories are pretty simple, but as your child gets older, the reading will become more complex. Characters will have more layers, and plots will be more involved. In order for your kid to keep up with a story, he will need to pay close attention to what's going on and draw conclusions along the way.

First things first: Get a sense of what your kid already knows. Turn the page and tell your kid to Jump Right In!

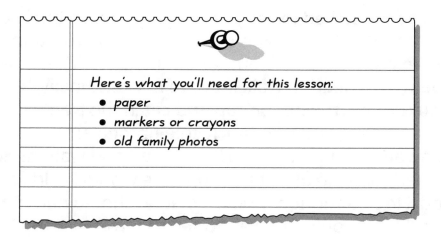

Here's what you'll need for this lesson:
- paper
- markers or crayons
- old family photos

 **Jump Right In!**

Read the story and answer the questions that follow.

Frog Trap

Richie was feeling lucky. Today he was going to catch a frog.

Richie walked to the pond with his net, a bucket, and a tub of flies. He was going to make a frog trap. He would need to lay the bucket on the grass. Then, the frog would need to walk into the bucket. Finally, he would throw the net on top and catch the frog.

It was a quiet morning. Richie tiptoed around the pond and set up his trap. He watched and waited. He started thinking about the home he would build for the frog. He also thought about what he should name the frog. Richie could not wait to see the frog!

1. What will Richie use to get the frog into the bucket?

    A. his finger

    B. a fish

    C. flies

2. Why do you think Richie is tiptoeing?

    A. because his feet hurt

    B. so he won't make any noise

    C. to scare the frog

3. What is Richie going to do with the frog?

Excellent Job!

Checking In

Ⓐ Answers for page 109:

    1. C

    2. B

    3. An A+ answer: "I think Richie is going to keep the frog as a pet."

Did your child get the correct answers? If so, ask your child to point out details from the story that support each answer.

Did your child get any of the answers wrong? Ask your child to explain the thinking behind each answer. Sometimes kids choose answers that might make sense but aren't supported by the story. For question 1, someone could use a finger to help guide the frog into the bucket, but there is nothing in the story that tells us that using a finger was the plan. Remind your child to choose the best answer based on clues from the story.

Watch Out!

Sometimes kids use their own experiences to draw their own conclusions rather than concrete details from the story. Your child might say that Richie is going to let the frog go because that's what your child would do. Although it's great that she is making a connection to the story, remind your kid that she shouldn't always assume that what happened in her life will happen in the story. Explain to your child that stories have details that give clues to help make conclusions. For example, in this story there is a detail that mentions Richie wanting to name the frog, and people usually name their pets.

What to Know...

Kids make conclusions about the world every day just by observing. Your child knows when you're in a good mood by the smile on your face. Your kid can also pick up on crying as a clue that someone is sad.

Review these skills with your child this way:

- A **conclusion** is an idea or thought based on facts.
- **Details** are bits of information in a passage. You can use the details in a passage to make a conclusion.

Your child can find details in illustrations to make conclusions.

· · · · · · · · · · · · · · ·

Ask your child to tell you a story based on the picture.

Most kids can use the details to tell you that a girl is having her birthday party.

Try to get your child to notice the more subtle details to draw some other conclusions.

- The girl is turning seven years old.
- The girl goes to Rosa Parks School.
- Someone got the birthday girl flowers.

 *Watch Out!*

Children not only use their own experiences to draw conclusions, they'll also draw conclusions based on their own wants. They may want the girl to be six, like them. Remind your child to use details based on the picture to draw a conclusion.

Your child can practice using details and drawing conclusions with these activities. You'll probably want to read these activities aloud to your child.

On Your Way to an "A" Activities

15 minutes

Type: Reading/Writing
Materials needed: pencils, paper, old family photos
Number of players: independent

You might have noticed that photos in a newspaper or magazine usually have a caption underneath describing what the picture is about. It's your turn to write captions for photos of you and your family! Choose a photo, preferably one you've never seen before. Use details from the photo to draw a conclusion about what is happening. Once you think you've figured it out, write a caption for this photo.

20 minutes

Type: Speaking/Listening
Materials needed: paper, markers or crayons
Number of players: 2

Go outside with someone in your family. Close your eyes. Listen to the sounds. What do you hear? Is there a truck passing? Is there a dog barking? What conclusions can you draw from the sounds in your neighborhood? Once you have a pretty good idea about what is happening in your neighborhood, go back into the house and draw what you heard on paper. Write a few sentences that tell what you think was happening.

Type: Arts and Crafts
Materials needed: paper, markers or crayons
Number of players: 4 or more

In "Pass the Crayon," players take turns adding details to a picture. Start with a blank sheet of paper. The first person will draw one thing. The next person will add something else, and so on. Once each person has added at least two details, take turns drawing conclusions and telling stories about the picture.

Type: Arts and Crafts
Materials needed: paper, markers or crayons
Number of players: independent

Walk into someone's bedroom in your house. Take a look around the room. What conclusions can you draw about that person? Use specific details to support your conclusions. What kind of room do you think your teacher might have? The person you sit next to in school? Your favorite book character? Draw what each person's bedroom would look like.

First Graders Are...

First graders can be moody. Sometimes they are not in the mood to do anything. If you find your child acting moody, don't force him or her to do something. Take a little break, and try some of these activities a bit later. You don't want your child to associate learning activities with negative feelings.

Has your child breezed through the activities? If so, he or she can work on this Using Your Head activity independently. You'll probably want to read the activity below aloud to your child.

Using Your Head

{ 15 minutes }

*Grab a **pencil**!*

Look at the picture of Richie and his frog. Answer the questions.

1. Do you think Richie will catch the frog with his net? Why or why not?

Answer: 1. No, because there's a big hole in the net.

Cracking the First Grade

Setting

Sometimes your kid is attentive to all the details of his surroundings. "Look, there's a ladybug," he might say in a garden full of colorful flowers. How did he notice that tiny detail in the setting? At other times, your kid might not notice a thing. "Where are we?" she might ask, having followed you around the mall and suddenly looking up. How did she manage to zone out?

Up until now, your child may or may not have noticed the setting in stories. But at this age, your child is ready to hone his ability to pick out details. By being able to pick out these details, your child is better able to communicate about the story. Your kid will be able to look back at what he read and describe the setting. And if after reading a story, your kid doesn't know the setting, then you and he will know that something is missing and that he needs to read the story again.

Setting is a great skill to practice in first grade. It requires your kid to think about what she read and to recall details. It also shows your kid that a story is supposed to give certain information. The setting influences the story in many ways: the tone, the characters, the plot. Think about it: What's a scary story without a haunted house? By understanding the setting, your child's overall understanding of a story can develop.

First things first: Get a sense of what your kid already knows. Turn the page and tell your kid to Jump Right In!

Here's what you'll need for this lesson:
- *markers or crayons*
- *paper*
- *note cards*
- *glue*
- *old magazines*

 **Jump Right In!**

Read the story and answer the questions that follow.

Gone Fishing

"It's the perfect day to catch some fish," said Christopher.

Christopher's dad was taking Christopher and his friend Arthur to the lake. The sun was shining, and the temperature was 80 degrees. There weren't many more days left before school started. Christopher and Arthur wanted to make sure they spent every last minute having fun.

Arthur had never been fishing before. "How do you catch them?" asked Arthur.

"I put a worm on the hook. Then, I put my fishing pole in the lake. I keep it very still, and the fish bites it!" said Christopher.

"What do you do with them?" Arthur asked.

"I put them in a bucket of water. Then I clean them. After that my dad cooks them on the grill. Fish tastes great!" Christopher answered.

Right as Christopher said that, he felt a tug on his line, and he pulled up a big fish. Then, Arthur's line got tight.

"Oh, my!" Arthur said. "I think I caught one too!"

"Pull it up," Christopher said. "Be careful."

At the end of the pole was a fish!

"I caught one!" Arthur yelled. "Did you see that?"

"Great!" said Christopher. "Now we both have lunch!"

1. What time of year is it?

   A. winter

   B. spring

   C. summer

2. What is something you might find at the lake?

Excellent Job!

 *Checking In*

❶Answers for page 117:

    1. C

    2. An A+ answer: "You might find a frog, trees, other people fishing, or a dock."

Did your child get the correct answers? If so, ask your child to tell you more about where the story takes place. Encourage your child to underline parts of the story that describe the setting.

Did your child get any of the answers wrong? If so, follow up each question with additional questions to help guide your child's thinking. For question 1, you could ask, "What was the weather like?" or "Were Christopher and Arthur in school?"

 *Watch Out!*

Your child may not have much prior experience with lakes and therefore might have trouble visualizing the setting. To help your kid, you may want to show him or her several pictures of lakes. Use the pictures to point out important things about lakes, such as the still water, the plants found near them, the fish that swim in them, the activities that happen by them, and so on. You can also have your child compare the pictures of lakes to the description of the lake in the story.

What to Know...

If your child has a good understanding of the setting in a story, he or she will have an easier time visualizing the story.

Review this skill with your child this way:

- The **setting** is when and where a story takes place.

Your child can practice identifying the setting using the following picture.

Ask your child any of the following questions to help him or her describe the setting: Is the setting inside or outside? What is the time of day? What is the season? What is the weather like?

 *Checking In*

Could your kid answer the questions? If so, encourage him to think about how it might feel there (cold, warm). Ask him about the smells he might smell there and the sounds he might hear. If your child is having trouble answering the questions, activate his prior knowledge by getting him to tell you everything he knows about farms. See if there are gaps in your kid's knowledge that you can fill.

Ask your child to pay attention to the setting as you read the following poem together.

The Surprise

My brother told me he had a surprise.
What could it be? I asked with wide eyes.
I grabbed at his arm,
I groaned and I grunted.
I went to his room,
For this prize I hunted.
Books, toys, dirty clothes, and more.
Everything was all over the floor,
But not the prize I was looking for.
My brother was laughing,
So I said, it's time for bed!
He couldn't stop laughing,
His face was so red.
In the end, I got my surprise.
A broken old pretzel,
I couldn't believe my own eyes.

Most kids can use details in the poem to identify the setting:

- The story takes place in a home, mostly in the brother's room.
- The brother's room is messy, with books, toys, and dirty clothes on the floor.
- The story takes place in the evening or at night because the storyteller is about to go to bed.

On Your Way to an "A" Activities

{ **20** minutes }

Type: Reading/Writing
Materials needed: pencil, markers or crayons, a note card
Number of players: independent

It's time to go on your dream vacation. Send someone a postcard from the place you would go on your dream vacation. It can be a real place or an imaginary place. On one side of your note card, draw a picture of the place. On the other side, write a note telling someone about the place you are visiting. What is the weather like? What time of year is it? What do the surroundings look like it? What kinds of things can you do at this place?

{ **20** minutes }

Type: Arts and Crafts
Materials needed: paper, old magazines, glue.
Number of players: independent

The seasons are an important part of story settings. Think about what kinds of things happen in the fall, winter, spring, and summer. Use one piece of paper for each season. Flip through old magazines to find pictures that go with each season. Cut these pictures out and glue them onto the correct paper to make a collage. For example, you could cut out a picture of a swimming pool or a popsicle for summer. You could also cut out a picture of someone skiing for winter, or different color leaves for fall. When you are done, ask someone at home to identify the correct season for each collage.

First Graders Are...

First graders tire easily. Don't try to do all of these activities at once. Ease into them one at a time.

Has your child breezed through the activities? If so, he or she can work on this Using Your Head activity independently. You'll probably want to read the activity below aloud to your child.

Using Your Head

*Grab a **pencil**!*

Reread the story "Gone Fishing." In the box below, draw a picture of the setting. Include as many details as possible.

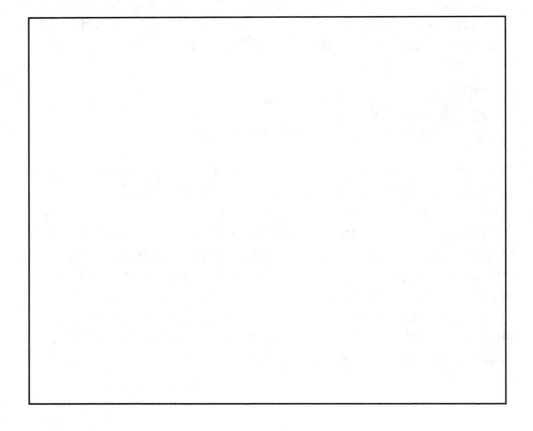

Answer: The picture could show a lake, a lot of greenery, the sun, two boys fishing, a father close by, a bucket, and fishing poles.

Characters

A big reason why your kid can become so engrossed with movies, TV shows, and books has to do with the characters. Sometimes it's because he can identify with a character. Maybe there's a first grader in his favorite TV show. Or maybe your kid plays the same sport as the main character in a book.

Although your kid probably has no problem telling you which character she likes or who her favorite superhero is, she might have trouble telling you why. Giving an explanation means your kid must describe this character. This doesn't mean just describing what this character looks like; it also means describing the character's personality. This often requires digging into the details of the story. For example, your child might infer that a character is nice because he shared his lunch with the new kid in school. The better your child understands characters, the better she will understand a story.

First things first: Get a sense of what your kid already knows. Turn the page and tell your kid to Jump Right In!

Here's what you'll need for this lesson:
- note cards
- children's book
- paper
- markers or crayons
- scissors
- tape
- popsicle sticks

Feel free to read the story and questions aloud.

 **Jump Right In!**

Read the story and answer the questions that follow.

The Game

Beaver snored. He was fast asleep. He loved to sleep. Then, his friend Squirrel came to his house by the river and woke him up.

Squirrel shouted, "Come on. Let's go to Rabbit's baseball game!"

Beaver yawned. He told Squirrel, "Don't bother me! I'm enjoying my sleep."

"Come on! You shouldn't be sleeping at 2:00 in the afternoon. You've missed all of Rabbit's baseball games. It will be fun! Trust me!" Squirrel said, as he started jumping on Beaver's bed.

Beaver rubbed his eyes. "All right. I will go," he said with a grunt. "I hope we don't have to walk far!"

They finally got to the game. Rabbit was up at bat. He hit the ball far.

Beaver yelled, "Wow, this is fun! I guess it's worth getting up early to have a good time with a good friend."

1. Who is one of the **main** characters in the story?
   A. Squirrel's brother
   B. the pitcher
   C. Beaver

2. Which best describes Beaver?
   A. mean
   B. lazy
   C. full of energy

3. How is Squirrel different from Beaver?

Excellent Job!

 *Checking In*

A Answers for page 125:

    1. C

    2. B

    3. An A+ answer: "Squirrel and Beaver are different because Beaver is very lazy and Squirrel has a lot of energy. Squirrel likes to be active. He likes going to games. Beaver just likes to sleep."

Did your child get the correct answers? If so, ask your child to support each answer with sentences from the story. You can also challenge your child to come up with more adjectives to describe Beaver and Squirrel.

Did your child get any of the answers wrong? If so, start by asking your child what the story was mostly about. Summarizing the story first can help your child recall details in order to answer the questions. If your child is having difficulty summarizing the story, reread the story aloud, and then ask your child the five Ws—who, what, when, where, and why. Help your child write the answers to each of the questions on a piece of paper. Your child can use these details to answer questions 1 through 3.

 *Watch Out!*

Question 3 might be tricky for the very literal mind of a first grader. Your child might answer with something like, "Squirrels and beavers are different animals" or "Beavers live in lodges, and squirrels live in trees." Although this information might be factually true, it is not specific to the story. Encourage your child to use information from the story to answer the question. Don't forget to praise your child for recalling such interesting facts about beavers and squirrels!

What to Know...

Characters make stories exciting. Your child can experience what a character sees, feels, wants, and thinks every time he reads a story!

Review these skills with your child this way:

- **Characters** are the people whose actions, ideas, thoughts, and feelings a story tells us about. Characters aren't always human. Sometimes animals, plants, or parts of the setting may be characters in a story.
- You can learn about a character through the **details** in a story, including what the character says and how the character behaves.

Your child can identify the characters in her favorite Saturday morning cartoon shows.

Ask your child to identify and describe the characters in one of his favorite TV shows. Ask questions like, "What does the character look like?" or "What do you know about the character's thoughts, ideas, and feelings?"

 *Watch Out!*

Your kid might have difficulty describing a character because she might be thinking about someone with a similar personality from her own life. Although it's great that your child can make connections between a story and her life, remind your child to support character descriptions with examples or details from the TV show or story.

Kids should be able to gather information about a character just by using the text.

Read the following story about Squirrel's friend Rabbit with your kid. Then, ask your child to describe Rabbit.

Rabbit was trying to go to bed, but he could not stop thinking about baseball. He couldn't wait for the next game. He had been practicing every day after school. Rabbit knew that all of this practice would help him hit a home run in the next game.

Most kids can use details in the story to describe Rabbit.

- He loves to play baseball.
- He works hard.
- He is sure of himself.

Remind your child to support his or her descriptions of Rabbit with text from the story.

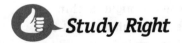 *Study Right*

Every time your child watches a movie or a TV show or reads a book, ask her to name her favorite character. Ask your child to tell you why and give at least three words to describe the character. This exercise can help build your child's adjective vocabulary.

Your child can practice describing characters with these activities. You'll probably want to read these activities aloud to your child.

On Your Way to an "A" Activities

 **{ 30 minutes }** Type: Game/Competitive
Materials needed: note cards, pencils, a children's book
Number of players: 4 or more

Read a good book with a few of your friends. Then, use note cards to write down the names of each character in the book. Next, mix the cards up and place the cards facedown on the table. Each player should pick a card without looking and tape it either to his or her forehead or back. Remember, don't look at the name! For the next 15 minutes, all of the players will talk to each other and treat each person as if he or she was actually the character whose name is on the card. Try to give clues and ask questions without ever saying the character's name. After 15 minutes, try to guess who you are, and then look at your card to see if you're right.

 **{ 25 minutes }** Type: Arts and Crafts
Materials needed: popsicle sticks or pencils, paper, markers or crayons, scissors, tape
Number of players: independent

You're going to put on a puppet show! First, think of the characters in your favorite story. What do they look like? Draw each character on a piece of paper. Then, cut each character out and tape it to a popsicle stick or a pencil. Get ready to retell the story using the puppets. Think about how the characters act. What kind of voice will each character have? How will you move each puppet? You are now ready for the puppet show! Don't forget to get behind a couch or a table so your audience can see only the puppets!

Using Your Head

{**10** minutes}

*Grab a **pencil**!*

Create a character poem about Beaver from the story "The Game" by filling in the blanks.

Beaver

Friends with _____

Lives by the _____

Likes to _____

Doesn't like to _____

Beaver

Create another character poem about a character from one of your favorite books. Start the poem by writing the character's name. Then, each line describes the character. Finally, end the poem with the character's name.

Answers: Squirrel, river, sleep, be active

Sequence

Your child probably knows that order matters: Wash your hands *before* you eat dinner. Dessert is allowed *after* you eat all of your vegetables. *First* finish your homework, and *then* you can play outside.

In school your child is also learning that order matters. The class might line up to go out to recess in a certain order, or put words in alphabetical order. Your child is also learning to pay attention to the order of events in a story.

Recognizing the order of events not only helps in reading comprehension, but it also helps kids break large tasks into smaller, more manageable tasks. For example, making a boat with building blocks might seem overwhelming for your child, but if he or she is given specific steps, it will probably be less daunting.

First things first: Get a sense of what your kid already knows. Turn the page and tell your kid to Jump Right In!

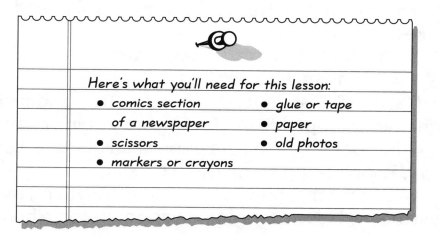

Here's what you'll need for this lesson:
- comics section of a newspaper
- scissors
- markers or crayons
- glue or tape
- paper
- old photos

Feel free to read the story and questions aloud.

 ## Jump Right In!

Read the story and answer the questions that follow.

The Pet Shop

Malik and Kristen walked quickly down the street with their mom. Today they were going to get a new pet.

They finally got to the pet shop. First, the kids saw kittens and puppies. Next, they saw frogs, fish, and snakes.

"I want that brown cat!" said Kristen.

"I want this green snake!" said Malik.

Malik and Kristen started to argue. Then suddenly, something stopped them. They heard yelping coming from the floor below. A cute puppy had gotten loose and was looking up at them and barking.

"We'll take that puppy," said Mom. "Anything that can stop my kids from fighting has got to come home with us."

Everyone went home very happy. They liked the trip to the pet shop.

1. What happened before the puppy started barking?

   A. Kristin, Malik, and their mom left the pet shop.

   B. The kids were fighting.

   C. Kristin, Malik, and their mom took the puppy home.

2. What did the kids see after they saw the kittens and puppies?

   A. turtles, lizards, and crabs

   B. birds and hamsters

   C. frogs, fish, and snakes

3. Retell the story by completing the sentences.

   First, _____

   Next, _____

   Finally, _____

Excellent Job!

 **Checking In**

◉Answers for page 133:

    1. B

    2. C

    3. An A+ answer: "First, Malik and Kristen walked to the pet shop. Next, Malik and Kristen argued about which pet to get. Finally, a barking dog interrupted their argument, and their mom decided to take home the dog."

Did your child get the correct answers? Check to see that it wasn't just a guess by asking your child to support his or her answers with sentences from the story.

Did your child get any of the answers wrong? If so, reread the story to your child, stopping after each important event in the story. After each time you stop, ask your child to draw a picture of what has happened so far. At the end, ask your child to retell the story using the pictures. Then, your child can use the pictures to give questions 1 through 3 another try.

 **Watch Out!**

Sometimes kids just get stressed out with multiple-choice questions. Try asking your child to retell the story before answering the questions. Then, ask your child to answer each question using his or her own words (not by choosing from one of the answer choices). Now, ask your child to find the answer choice that is most similar. Often, kids know the answers but the answer choices confuse them.

What to Know...

Sequencing is not just a reading skill. It can easily be applied to other parts of your child's everyday life.

Review these skills with your child this way:

- **Sequence** is the order of ideas and events in a story.
- You can describe the order of events using words such as *before*, *after*, *first*, *next*, *then*, or *last*.

When your kid does chores, he or she has to make sure things are done in order.

Ask your child to look at the pictures and tell what is happening in order. Remind your child to use order words such as *first, next,* and *last.* Encourage your child to use order words to tell you how other activities are completed.

 *Checking In*

Could your child use order words to describe the correct order of an activity? If so, ask your kid to tell you more details about the activity. What could have happened before the first step? What will happen after the last step? Encourage your child to vary his use of order words. For example, your child can use *finally* instead of *last*.

Making a peanut butter and jelly sandwich requires your child to follow steps in a specific order.

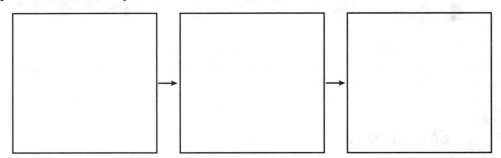

Ask your child to use order words to explain how to make a peanut butter and jelly sandwich.

Checking In

If your child is having trouble describing how to make a peanut butter and jelly sandwich in order, grab some bread, peanut butter, jelly, a plate, and a knife, and have your child actually make a peanut butter and jelly sandwich! Tell your child to describe each step as she does it.

In school, your child might be learning how to use sequencing maps to help him or her place events in a story in the correct order.

Your child can use this type of sequencing map after he finishes a good book. Have your child write down the important events in order, using one box for each event. You can also have your child draw a picture for each event instead of using words.

Study Right

Whenever possible, ask your kid to tell you about her day, starting from the beginning. Remind your child to use words like *first, next, then,* and *finally* when telling about her day.

Your child can practice sequencing with these activities. You'll probably want to read these activities aloud to your child.

On Your Way to an "A" Activities

20 minutes

Type: Game/Competitive
Materials needed: comics section of the newspaper, paper, scissors, glue or tape
Number of players: 2

Each person will cut out his or her favorite comic strip from the newspaper. Next, each person will cut out each frame of the strip so the pictures are no longer connected. Then, shuffle the pictures and exchange them with your partner. You and your partner will have to figure out the correct order of the frames. Glue or tape the pictures back together in the correct order and ask your partner to check to see if you are correct.

25 minutes

Type: Reading/Writing
Materials needed: pencil, paper, markers or crayons, old photos, glue or tape
Number of players: 2

Put together a timeline that describes your life. For each year of your life, write down one important event that happened. You can illustrate the events or glue pictures of yourself at that age to the timeline. Ask your parents for help to tell you about years that you may not remember. Next, use the timeline to tell someone at home your life story, starting from birth. Don't forget to use sequence words!

First Graders Are...

First graders like to have a defined space in which to work. Make sure you have a space in your house set aside for your child to work on these activities, with materials readily available.

Has your child breezed through the activities? If so, he or she can work on this Using Your Head activity independently. You'll probably want to read the activity below aloud to your child.

Using Your Head

{ **15** minutes }

*Grab a **pencil**!*

Read the next part of the story "The Pet Shop" below. Then, draw pictures to show the order of what happened in this part of the story.

Malik and Kristen had to get their house ready for their new dog. First, their mom helped them fill up food and water dishes. Then, Kristen laid out the dog bed they bought at the pet shop. Next, Malik set out all of the dog toys they picked out. Now that the house was ready, Malik and Kristen brought the dog outside to play fetch.

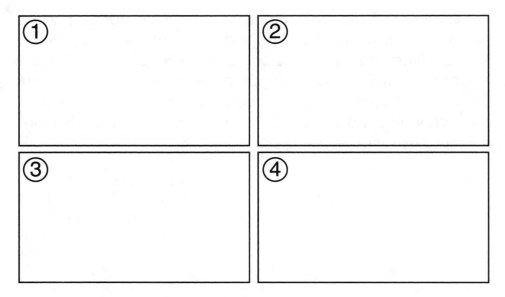

Answers: First: filling up food and water dishes; second: laying out the dog bed; third: laying out dog toys; fourth: playing fetch outside

Plot

It's what makes your child root for the good guy and boo the bad guy in her favorite TV show. It's what makes your kid cover his eyes and jump at the tiniest sound when he's watching a scary movie. It's what gets your kid's adrenaline pumping when her favorite book character is about to open the door that leads to danger. A good plot draws your child into a TV show, movie, or book.

The term *plot* might be new and abstract for your child. In first grade, your child might be comfortable telling what happens in a story, but understanding plot is different from giving a quick summary. Plot involves the structure of a story and how the events in a story are related. Once your child sees how everything is connected, his reading comprehension will improve and his sense of the story will be stronger. Paying attention to plot will help your child be in control of his reading experience.

First things first: Get a sense of what your kid already knows. Turn the page and tell your kid to Jump Right In!

Here's what you'll need for this lesson:
- *paper*

 **Jump Right In!**

Read the story and answer the questions that follow.

Missing Cat!

Jasmine was ready for a great Sunday afternoon. She brought her favorite book and her cat, Freckles, out to her backyard. She put her book down and played with Freckles. He loved to be chased! After a little while, Jasmine became tired. It was time to read her book. She found a nice spot of grass to sit on and began to read. After Jasmine finished her book, she decided it was time to go inside for lunch. The only problem was that she couldn't find Freckles.

She looked everywhere. He wasn't by the gate or the picnic table. Jasmine was very worried.

All of a sudden, Jasmine heard a soft, scratching sound in the yard. Was it Freckles? She listened more closely and heard that the noise was coming from up above. Jasmine looked up, and there was Freckles in the tree, looking very scared. Finally, Freckles was found!

1. In the middle of the story, what made Jasmine worried?

    A. She could not find her favorite book.

    B. She could not find her cat.

    C. It looked like it was about to rain.

2. What clue did Jasmine use to find Freckles?

    A. She heard sounds from inside her house.

    B. She saw Freckles's tail by the gate.

    C. She heard scratching sounds coming from a tree.

3. Which part of the story made you nervous?

Excellent Job!

 *Checking In*

Answers for page 141:

    1. B

    2. C

    3. An A+ answer: "I was nervous when Jasmine realized her cat was missing. I also was nervous when she first heard noises."

Did your child get the correct answers? If so, ask your child to tell you what happened in the story, from beginning to end. Check to see that your child is using details, rather than giving a quick summary. Ask your child questions like, "What is the problem in the story?" and "How did the problem happen?" and "How did the problem get solved?"

Did your child get any of the answers wrong? If so, check to see if your child understood the story by asking him or her to give you a quick summary. Then ask your child to reread the story, stopping every so often to tell you what has happened. This will help your child pay attention to the plot development. Have your child take another try at answering the questions.

 *Watch Out!*

This might be the first time that your child has looked for a problem in a story. Help your child understand this term by giving some examples of problems and solutions from his or her life. Perhaps your kid and his brother argued about the TV show they wanted to watch. How did this problem get solved?

What to Know...

The characters, the setting, exciting events, problems, and the solution all contribute to a story's plot.

Review this skill with your child this way:

- The **plot** is the series of events in a fictional story.

Read the following story with your kid.

Isaac's Ice Cream

Isaac was standing outside of his house on a hot summer day. He was holding an ice-cream cone. All of a sudden, he felt something wet running down his arm. He looked down, and there were green drops all over his shoes. His ice cream was melting all over! It was a mess! Isaac needed to do something quick, or there wouldn't be any ice cream left in his cone. Lucky for him, his mom came out with a bowl. Isaac put the ice-cream cone in the bowl. His ice cream was saved!

Ask your child to tell you about the plot of this story. Make sure your child includes what happened in the beginning, middle, and end; recognizes the exciting parts leading up to the problem; and identifies the problem and solution.

Most kids can do a pretty good job of telling you what happened in the beginning, middle, and end:

- Beginning—Isaac was eating ice cream on a hot, sunny day.
- Middle—Isaac's ice cream started to melt and get messy.
- End—Isaac's mom brought out a bowl to save the ice cream.

 ## Checking In

Breaking down the story into beginning, middle, and end will push your child to describe the events using details. Otherwise, your child might give you a quick sentence to describe what happened.

Most kids can identify the exciting parts in the story by thinking about the part that made him or her worried:

- the ice cream melting
- the ice cream making a mess, dripping on Isaac's arm and shoes

Most kids can use the exciting part to figure out the problem and the solution:

- The ice cream was melting, and soon Isaac would not have any ice cream left. It would be all over the ground.
- Isaac's mom brought out the bowl to save the ice cream.

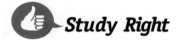 ## Study Right

When your child is telling you about something, make sure you follow up with a lot of "why" and "how" questions. The more detailed your child is at describing his or her own life, the more details and events your kid will notice when reading stories.

Your child can practice identifying the plot with these activities. You'll probably want to read these activities aloud to your child.

On Your Way to an "A" Activities

 **20** **minutes**
Type: Reading/Writing
Materials needed: pencils, paper
Number of players: 4 or more

Build a story with your friends! The only thing you need to do together is decide on a problem for the story. Once you have a problem, you can begin. The first player starts the story by writing the first sentence. Next, pass the pencil and paper to the next person, who will add the next sentence, and so on. Remember, don't get to the problem right away. Keep passing the paper until you have all the elements of a good story, including a great beginning, middle, and end; a problem; and a solution.

 **20** **minutes**
Type: Speaking/Listening
Materials needed: none
Number of players: 2

Play "What would you do if...?" Each player thinks of a problem he or she might have. It can be a small problem, like having an untied shoe, or a big problem, like getting into an argument with an older brother or seeing someone cheat on a test. Tell your problem to your partner, and ask your partner to come up with a solution. Take turns giving problems and solutions.

First Graders Are...
At this time in their lives, first graders are already searching for connections outside of their families. Friendships are very important. Your child might be more apt to enjoy these activities if he or she can do them with a friend. Encourage your kid to invite friends over to take part in these practice activities.

Has your child breezed through the activities? If so, he or she can work on this Using Your Head activity independently. You'll probably want to read the activity below aloud to your child.

Using Your Head

{15 minutes}

*Grab a **pencil**!*

Draw what happened in the beginning, middle, and end of "Missing Cat!" Draw the most exciting part of the story.

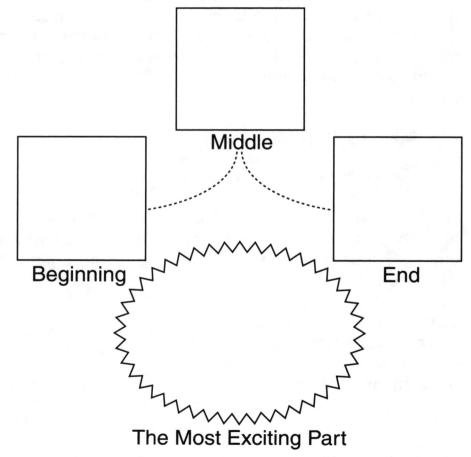

Middle

Beginning

End

The Most Exciting Part

Answers: Beginning—Jasmine goes outside to play with her cat and read a book. Middle—Jasmine realizes that she has lost her cat. End—Jasmine finds her cat in the tree. The Most Exciting Part—Jasmine hears scratching noises.

Numbers to 100

Most children have been using numbers since they were toddlers. When your child asked for one more cracker at lunch or when you hoisted your children onto your lap to count the animals in a favorite board book for the hundredth time, the world of numbers was informally introduced.

Now that your child is in school, numbers are being explored and expanded in a more formal way. Think of those early experiences with numbers as the foundation of a house. Now it is time to help construct the frame and, as your child gains knowledge and practice, nail on the boards. Help your kid build upon her early experiences and approach new challenges with confidence.

Notice how your child plays a board game. Does she have to count each dot on the die to find the number rolled or does she "just know" it is a three? Can your child jump her piece ahead three spaces or does she have to count each space? This is an important distinction. When your child "just knows" that the die says five or can easily hop ahead five spaces on the game board, you know that she is developing her number sense. The activities that follow, as well as everyday experiences that you and your kid have with numbers, will go far in strengthening her foundations in math.

First things first: Get a sense of what your kid already knows. Turn the page and tell your kid to Jump Right In!

Here's what you'll need for this lesson:

- *paper*
- *markers or crayons*
- *calendar*
- *modeling clay or dough*
- *paper plate*
- *box or basket*

Feel free to read the questions aloud.

Jump Right In!

1. How many crackers are on the plate above?

   A. 5

   B. 10

   C. 12

   D. 26

2. Which number comes next?

   43, 44, 45, 46, 47, ____

   A. 46

   B. 50

   C. 84

   D. 48

3. Help the space shuttle blast off! Count backward from 10. Write in the missing numbers.

10, 9, 8, 7, _____, _____, 4, 3, _____,

_____, _____

4. The space shuttle crew saw 17 meteors. Draw 17 meteors.

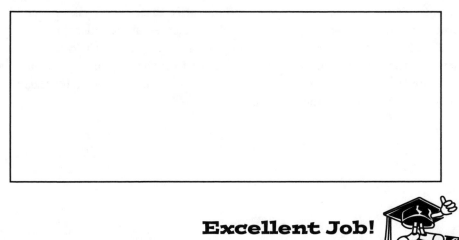

Excellent Job!

 *Checking In*

Ⓐ Answers for pages 150 and 151:

    1. C

    2. D

    3. An A+ answer: 6, 5, and 2, 1, 0

    4. An A+ answer: A picture of 17 meteors

Did your child get the correct answers? If so, you could say, "Show me how you count." Your child can use his fingers or count in his head. With the drawings, your child can count by pointing to each item or crossing out each item after it's been counted.

Did your child get any of the answers wrong? If so, ask, "What did you do to get that answer?" Help your child count each object by pointing to each picture and counting together. If she gets confused, show her how to cross out each object as it is counted. If your child has trouble counting by ones with larger numbers, remind her that each number will be one more than the last number she said.

 *Watch Out!*

First graders are more familiar with writing, reading, and saying numbers from 0 to 10 than with numbers greater than 10. Also, your child may still need practice with counting transitions, for example, 19 to 20, 29 to 30, and so on.

Use your family calendar to help your child practice these skills. Ask your child to point to the numbers you say. Have your child practice saying numbers by calling out numbers for you to find. Ask your child to read the numbers on the calendar in order, then read them backward. Have your child start from the last number on the calendar and write the numbers that come after it when counting up to 50 or 100. Look for patterns in the numbers and talk about them.

What to Know...

Your child is learning to read, write, say, and count numbers from 0 to 100.

Your child could use these skills to find a friend's house number when going to a birthday party.

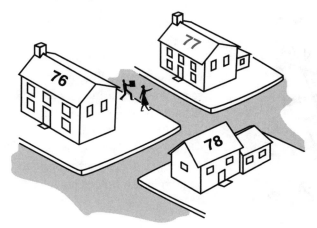

Ask your child to identify the house numbered 77. Then, ask your child to find numbers between 0 and 100 around the house and read them to you. Direct him to kitchen appliances, food packages, magazines, and so on. Have your child make a list of all the numbers he can find in five minutes.

Your child might want to count the number of seashells in his or her collection.

Encourage your child to count the seashells aloud. Have your child cross out or mark each seashell as it is counted to help keep track.

 **Watch Out!**

If your child gets "stuck" while counting, help your kid by "backing up" to help jog his or her memory. For example, if your child can't remember the number 20, say, "17, 18, 19, now what comes next?"

When playing games like hide-and-seek, your child might need to count back from 100.

...3, 2, 1.
Ready or not,
here I come!

Play games with your child that require counting, including counting backward. Encourage your child to say the numbers aloud so that he can hear his mistakes if he makes some. Help your kid increase his counting speed when counting forward by saying: "How high can you count while I take out the garbage or while you put on your shoes?" Repeat the activity often so that your child can see his progress.

 ## Checking In

Is your child mixing up digits when saying or writing the numbers? Remind your child that reading and writing numbers is like reading and writing words; they always go from left to right. Say a number, such as "sixty-one." Write the number as you say it. Say it again. Have your child point to the number 6 as you say "sixty" and the number 1 as you say "one."

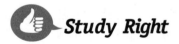 ## Study Right

Help your child make a 100-chart. Make a 10-square-by-10-square grid on a piece of paper. Have your child write the number 1 in the top left square and then write the numbers in order to 10 to fill in the rest of the row. Ask your child to continue writing the numbers in order to 100, starting at the left of the next row and moving to the right. Help him or her with any errors. Next, have your kid look at the 100-chart and find any patterns. Talk about how all the numbers in the second column are numbers that end in 2, for example. Say the numbers aloud in the column, then point to each number as you say it. This will help your child match the number she hears with the number she sees and prevent mistakes like writing 601 for 61. Let your child use the 100-chart as a reference while working on other activities in this book.

Your child can practice reading, writing, saying, counting, and using numbers to describe sets of objects with these activities. You'll probably want to read these activities aloud to your child.

On Your Way to an "A" Activities

 **15 minutes**
Type: Active
Materials needed: box or basket, paper, pencil
Number of players: 2

Have a counting scavenger hunt. One person is the Leader and the other person is the Hunter. The Leader asks the Hunter to find a number of objects in the house or yard. The Leader might say, "Find 25 pebbles." The Hunter finds the pebbles and puts them in the box or basket. The Hunter and the Leader count the pebbles. If the Hunter found the correct number of pebbles, the Leader and Hunter switch places and play again using a new number and a different object.

 **20 minutes**
Type: Arts and Crafts
Materials needed: modeling clay or dough, paper plate
Number of players: 2 or more

Play with your favorite numbers. Find numbers like your house number, your dog's age, or the number of pages in your favorite book. Choose three numbers to sculpt out of clay or dough. Display them on a paper plate. Tell someone at home where you found the numbers and why they are important to you.

Has your child breezed through the activities? If so, he or she can work on this Using Your Head activity independently. You may want to read the activity below aloud to your child.

Using Your Head

{ **20** minutes }

*Grab some **markers** or **crayons**!*

Read aloud all the numbers in the picture below. Look at the key to match the numbers to a color. Then, color. What shape do you see?

25 = green	74 = purple	37 = orange
96 = blue	89 = red	62 = yellow

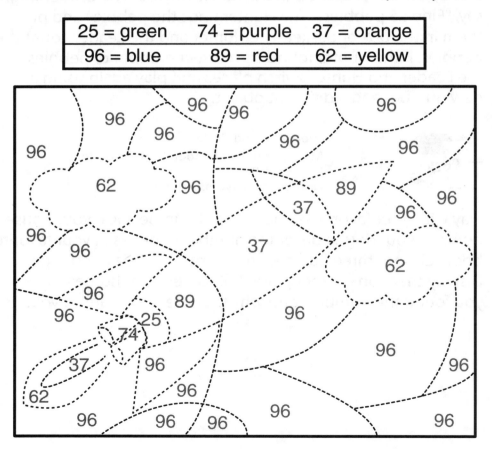

Answer: After coloring, a rocket will appear.

Place Value and the Base-Ten System

Kids who are confident with reading and writing numbers may "hit the wall" when it comes to place value. This is a new way for your child to think about numbers. It may be difficult to grasp that a digit can have a different value depending on its place. Even more difficult to understand is that two numbers can use the same digits (54 and 45), yet have different values.

Your kid doesn't have to develop some highfalutin', philosophical understanding of numbers at this age. But soon enough, she will need to know how to regroup in order to add and subtract large numbers. She'll also need to know how to make change and how to convert when measuring. These are skills vital in math class and in other subjects. These are also skills your child will want and need as she grows up. But for now, keep it simple and focus only on helping your child get a basic understanding of the tens and ones places. Once your kid feels comfortable with this skill, she will be ready for other skills to come.

First things first: Get a sense of what your kid already knows. Tell your kid to turn the page and Jump Right In!

Here's what you'll need for this lesson:
- *paper*
- *markers or crayons*
- *deck of cards*
- *muffin pan*
- *cereal squares, raisins, and pretzel sticks*
- *dice*

Feel free to read the questions aloud.

Jump Right In!

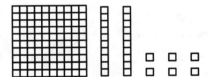

1. What number is shown by the base-ten blocks?

    A. 5

    B. 54

    C. 40

    D. 45

2. What number is shown by the base-ten blocks?

    A. 62

    B. 162

    C. 126

    D. 26

3. What number is in the tens place?

hundreds	tens	ones
1	7	8

A. 7

B. 8

C. 1

D. 0

4. Write a number that has an 8 in the tens place.

hundreds	tens	ones

5. Circle the number in the ones place. Underline the number in the tens place. Draw a box around the number in the hundreds place.

139

Excellent Job!

 *Checking In*

A Answers for pages 158 and 159:

   1. D

   2. C

   3. A

   4. An A+ answer: Your child should write a three-digit number, such as 189.

   5. An A+ answer: Your child should circle the nine, underline the three, and box the one.

Did your child get the correct answers? You could say, "Show me how you counted the blocks" or "What does each type of block stand for?"

Did your child get any of the answers wrong? Help your child to identify each type of block. The smallest block is called a "unit," and it stands for 1. The tall, skinny block is called a "long," and it stands for 10. The flat, square block is called a "flat," and it stands for 100. Count each type of block in questions 1 and 2 with your child and say the value aloud. In question 1, count the longs first and say, "10, 20, 30, 40. 4 tens." In question 3, if your kid was confused by the place-value chart, read the labels over each column on the chart. Then, point to each number in the chart as you say, "1 hundred, 7 tens, 8 ones, or 178."

 *Watch Out!*

First graders who are just beginning to understand place value may get hung up when a number contains a zero. Show your child how to draw a place-value chart (like the chart in question 4) around the number. Remind him or her that a zero in the ones place just means that the number has no ones, as in the number 70. Show your child that zero is still an important placeholder. If it wasn't there, 70 would be 7!

Choose a few important numbers, like family birth dates, and write one digit each on an index card. From left to right, lay out an index card labeled 100s, an index card labeled 10s, and an index card labeled 1s. Mix up the digit cards and have your child arrange them under the place-value cards to show important numbers. For example, if your kid's birthday is August 20, he or she would put the number 2 card under the tens and the number 0 card under the ones. Have your child tell how many hundreds, tens, and ones are in each number.

What to Know...

In school, your child will learn about place value. Your child will learn about the ones place, the tens place, and the hundreds place.

Review these skills with your child this way:

- A **digit** is a symbol that is used to write numbers. There are 10 digits: 0, 1, 2, 3, 4, 5, 6, 7, 8, and 9.
- **Place value** is the value of a digit based on its place in a number. For example, in the number 382, the digit 8 is in the tens place, so it has a value of 80.

Your child uses place value when building a model with interlocking blocks.

hundreds	tens	ones
3	2	5

325 blocks

Ask your child to tell you how many blocks are in the box. Discuss how many hundreds, tens, and ones are in the number. Next, create a place-value chart. Hold a piece of paper horizontally and fold it to make three equal sections. Write "hundreds," "tens," and "ones" from left to right at the top of each section. Find other groups of objects around the house for your child to count, then have your kid write the number in the place-value chart.

A teacher might use place value to help with organizing supplies.

Ask your child, "How many pencils are there?" Draw a place-value chart and have your child write the number 19. Ask your child, "Which digit shows how many tens? Which digit shows how many ones?" Rearrange the digits to show the number 91. Talk about how the value of the number has changed.

 ## Checking In

Is your child writing a two-digit number in the hundreds, tens, or ones column? Use a three-by-four-hole muffin pan to make a place-value chart. Cover the pan with a piece of foil so that only three holes are showing. These will stand for the hundreds, tens, and ones places. Write three sets of the numbers 0 through 9 on muffin papers with a marker. Say a number, such as 159. Have your child arrange the muffin papers in the pan to show the number. Remind your child that just as only one muffin paper fits in each hole in the pan, only one digit fits into each place in the chart.

First Graders Are...

Even though your child is beginning to learn abstract concepts, children of this age still enjoy and need many opportunities to work with these skills by using concrete materials like base-ten blocks; small items to count and group like pebbles, paper clips, or raisins; and visual organizers like place-value charts.

Your child can practice place value with these activities. You'll probably want to read these activities aloud to your child.

On Your Way to an "A" Activities

15 minutes

Type: Game/Competitive
Materials needed: 3 dice, pretzel sticks, raisins, cereal squares
Number of players: 1 or more

Play a game and eat it too! Divide the snacks among the players, then have each player sort the items into three separate piles. Think of the food snacks as base-ten blocks, where the raisins stand for ones, the pretzel sticks for tens, and the cereal squares for hundreds. Roll two dice, show that number using the base-ten snacks, then eat them! For example, if you roll a 26, you would take two pretzel sticks (2 tens) and six raisins (6 ones). For an added challenge, use three dice and cereal squares to make and eat three-digit numbers.

10 minutes

Type: Reading/Writing
Materials needed: deck of cards (10s and face cards removed), paper, pencil
Number of players: 1

Place the deck of cards facedown. Draw three cards and lay them side by side. Think of the numbers shown as a three-digit number. Have your parent or friend help you draw a place-value chart. Read the number shown by the cards and write it in the correct columns on the chart. Mix up the three cards. Read and write the new number in the chart. How many different numbers can you make with the same three cards?

Has your child breezed through the activities? If so, he or she can work on this Using Your Head activity independently. You may want to read the activity below aloud to your child.

Using Your Head

{ **10** minutes }

*Grab a **pencil**!*

Write a three-digit number in the place-value chart below, then say the number aloud.

hundreds	tens	ones

Now, draw a picture of objects to show the value of the digit in the tens place.

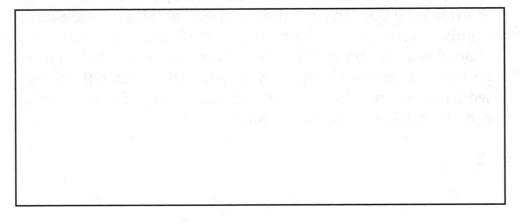

Grouping Tens and Ones

Children see the world simply. If two things are the same, they expect them to look the same. If two things are different, they expect them to look different. This is often why kids get confused when working with base-ten blocks. In school your kid will learn that 1 ten equals 10 ones, but the base-ten blocks used to represent each look very different. A long is used to represent 1 ten, and it looks like a tall, thin bar. Ten units are used to represent 10 ones. Units are separate, little cubes. It may begin to make sense once the units are placed in a row. Then, these 10 units actually do resemble 1 long. All in all, these new concepts can be quite puzzling.

Once your child has a better handle on tens and ones, he or she will learn how to trade in 10 ones for 1 ten. Once grouping tens and ones becomes crystal clear, adding and subtracting larger numbers will make more sense for your child.

First things first: Get a sense of what your kid already knows. Tell your kid to turn the page and Jump Right In!

Here's what you'll need for this lesson:

- *markers or crayons*
- *paper*
- *rubber bands*
- *silverware*
- *grid paper*
- *paper clips*
- *die*
- *box*

Feel free to read the questions aloud.

Jump Right In!

1.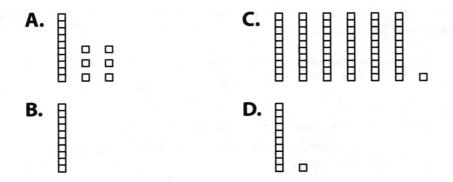

Which picture below shows the same number as the picture above?

A.

C.

B.

D.

2. Count by 10s. What number is missing?

10, 20, _____, 40, 50

A. 0

B. 1

C. 21

D. 30

Cracking the First Grade

3. May showed the number 40 below.

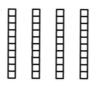

Which of the following is true?

A. 4 tens = 4 ones

B. 4 tens = 40 ones

C. 4 tens = 400 ones

D. 4 tens = 4 hundreds

4. Circle groups of 10 strawberries.

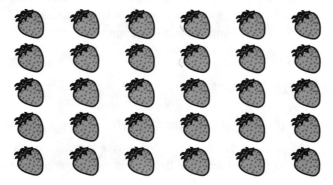

5. Jamal got 23 single baseball cards for his birthday. Draw a picture to show the baseball cards in groups of tens and ones.

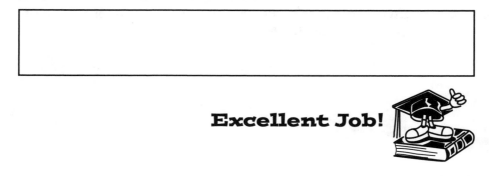

Excellent Job!

 **Checking In**

A Answers for pages 166 and 167:

1. A
2. D
3. B
4. An A+ answer: Your child should circle 3 groups of 10.
5. An A+ answer: Your child should draw 2 groups of 10 cards and 3 individual cards.

Did your child get the correct answers? You could say, "Show me how you group by tens" or "Show me how you count by tens and ones." You can also ask your child to tell you the number represented in each of the answer choices for questions 1 and 3.

Did your child get any of the answers wrong? Help your child see how organizing and counting groups of objects by tens is a quick way to find out how many objects are in a set. Compare a base-ten rod with the circled group of strawberries and 10 units. Show how each stands for 10, even though they are arranged differently.

 **Watch Out!**

Kids still get confused about the similarities and differences between 1 ten and 10 ones. Tell your kid that trading 10 ones for 1 ten is like organizing his bedroom. Ask him to imagine that books are all over his floor. This makes his books messy and hard to find. Now, have him imagine his books stacked across his bookshelf in piles of 10. There is the same number of books, but they are ordered in a neat and more manageable way.

Help your child to start thinking in tens. Give her a tray of silverware and have her group the forks into coffee mugs by tens. Encourage your child to count the forks before and after she groups them. Help her see how the number of forks didn't change when the forks were organized differently.

What to Know...

In school, your child will learn that 10 ones is the same as 1 ten. Your child will learn how to use these concepts for addition and subtraction.

Your child groups by tens and ones when putting crayons back into their box.

Ask your child to tell you how many crayons are in the picture. Ask your child, "Can you make a set of 10 crayons with the crayons left over to place in the box? Why not? How many more crayons will you need to find to make a set of 10?" Now, let your child loose on the "junk drawer," change jar, or a messy closet at home. Have her organize items into piles of tens and ones. When your kid has made a group of ten separate items, have her bundle or bag them into tens. Your child is also learning that 10 tens is the same as 1 hundred. So, when your kid has 10 tens, have her bundle them into 1 hundred.

A builder uses grouping to organize his supplies when they are delivered to the worksite.

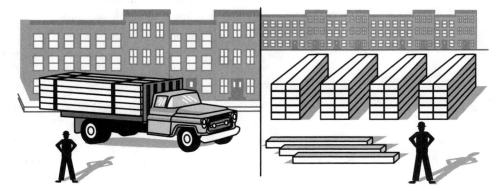

Ask your child to count the pieces of wood by tens and ones. How many were delivered to the builder? How did the builder group the pieces of wood?

Checking In

If your child is confused by the concept of grouping, remind him that he has the keys to the kingdom right at the ends of his arms: his fingers! Have your child hold up both hands and make fists. Have him count by ones to 10 by holding up one finger at a time as he counts. Remind your child that he counted 10 ones. Now, have your child put his hands by his sides. Ask him to "flash ten" by holding out his hands with all his fingers up and shouting "ten" to count 1 ten. Continue by adding your own fingers to the mix to make numbers 11 through 20. Count them by ones, then by tens with the flashing method.

Study Right

Your child can use grid paper to make his or her own version of base-ten blocks. Fold the grid paper in half vertically. On the left side, color in a random assortment of squares—say 37. Ask your child to count the squares by ones, then write the number below the drawing. On the right side, ask your kid to show that number by coloring in columns of 10 grid squares for tens, and single grid squares for ones. This is a visual way for your child to practice grouping. After your child has completed several of these, staple them together to make a book for your child to reference as needed.

First Graders Are...

Your child will feel more comfortable using objects, props, and pictures to demonstrate these skills before she can attempt these types of exercises in her head. It is natural for first graders to fall back on using their fingers to count and group. As your kid gains experience and confidence, you will see her make a subtle shift to "mental math" when figuring out problems.

Your child can practice place value with these activities. You'll probably want to read these activities aloud to your child.

On Your Way to an "A" Activities

Type: Game/Competitive
Materials needed: none
Number of players: 3 or more

Play "Friend, May I?" Choose one person to be the "friend." Have the friend stand at one end of the driveway or playground and face the players standing at the other end. A player chooses a number from 10 to 50 and asks to count. For example, "Friend, may I count to 25?" Then, count by 10s and take one hop forward for each 10. Take 1 step forward for each 1. So, for 25, you would take 2 hops and 5 steps. Remember, hops are with both feet! The friend can send the player back to the start if the player miscounts, missteps, or forgets to say, "Friend, may I?" The first player to reach the friend wins the game!

Type: Game/Competitive
Materials needed: paper clips, box, die
Number of players: 1 or more

Each player creates five paper clip chains by connecting 10 paper clips for each chain. Now there should be 5 sets of tens. Put the 5 tens in a special box. Take turns rolling the die and taking that many single paper clips from the paper clip container. Continue rolling and taking paper clips from the paper clip container until you have 10 single paper clips and can trade them for one of the tens in the special box. The first person to collect 50 paper clips (5 tens) wins the game!

Has your child breezed through the activities? If so, he or she can work on this Using Your Head activity independently. You may want to read the activity below aloud to your child.

Using Your Head

{ 30 minutes }

*Grab some **markers** or **crayons**!*

You are in charge of sorting out the sticker box at the toy store.

Draw the following stickers:

35 yellow smiley face stickers

22 red heart stickers

3 purple triangle stickers

Now, circle groups of 10 stickers. Make sure each group has the same kind of sticker. How many stickers are there in all? _____

Answer: 3 groups of 10 yellow faces and 5 other yellow smiley faces; 2 groups of 10 red hearts and 2 other red hearts; and 3 purple triangles drawn; 60 stickers in all

Addition

Your child has probably been using addition concepts since he was very young without even knowing it. Maybe your child used blocks to build block towers, and then later decided to use extra blocks to make the tower taller. Or he might have taken one cookie from the cookie jar, and then, feeling a bit unsatisfied, decided to have one more. Your kid could tell you that he ate two cookies in all.

In school, your child might be slightly puzzled by the introduction of the plus sign and the equal sign, and how these signs relate to what she already understands about addition. For example, she can easily add her four stuffed animals to her friend's three stuffed animals, and know that she is playing with seven stuffed animals in all, but in school she might be confused when asked to solve 4 + 3. There are a lot of basic addition facts to be learned in first grade. Knowing these facts will set your child up for success in elementary school, especially as your kid starts to add larger numbers and to multiply. For now, build the foundation for strong math skills by helping your child connect what she knows about combining objects, such as toys or snacks, to the symbols used to represent addition and to solve addition facts.

First things first: Get a sense of what your kid already knows. Turn the page and tell your kid to Jump Right In!

Here's what you'll need for this lesson:
- *markers or crayons*
- *paper*
- *stapler*
- *glitter glue, fuzzy stickers, or dried beans*
- *highlighter pens*
- *masking tape*
- *deck of cards*

Feel free to read the questions aloud.

 **Jump Right In!**

Use the addition facts table below to answer the questions.

+	0	1	2	3	4	5	6	7	8	9
0	0	1	2	3	4	5	6	7	8	9
1	1	2	3	4	5	6	7	8	9	10
2	2	3	4	5	6	7	8	9	10	11
3	3	4	5	6	7	8	9	10	11	12
4	4	5	6	7	8	9	10	11	12	13
5	5	6	7	8	9	10	11	12	13	14
6	6	7	8	9	10	11	12	13	14	15
7	7	8	9	10	11	12	13	14	15	16
8	8	9	10	11	12	13	14	15	16	17
9	9	10	11	12	13	14	15	16	17	18

1. $5 + 5 =$

   A. 5

   B. 8

   C. 9

   D. 10

2. $7 + 2 =$

   A. 8

   B. 9

   C. 11

   D. 12

3. 3 + 8 =

   A. 7

   B. 9

   C. 10

   D. 11

4. 6 + 7 =

   A. 9

   B. 10

   C. 12

   D. 13

5. Draw a picture to show the answer to the addition fact.

$$13 + 4 =$$

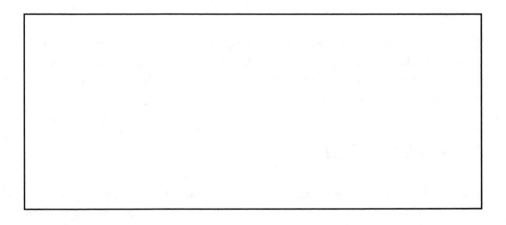

6. There are 7 crayons in a box. Write an addition fact that equals 7.

_____ + _____ = _____

Excellent Job!

Checking In

ⒶAnswers for pages 174 and 175:

1. D
2. B
3. D
4. D
5. An A+ answer: A group of 17 items are drawn.
6. An A+ answer: A fact with the sum of 7 will be written, such as 4 + 3 = 7 or 5 + 2 = 7.

Did your child get the correct answers? You could say, "Show me how you used the addition facts table to get the answers" or "Tell me what the plus sign and the equal sign mean."

Did your child get any of the answers wrong? Read an addition fact aloud with your child. Use a highlighter to highlight each addend (the numbers added). Then, highlight down the column and across the row to find the sum on the facts table. Say the fact again, this time with the sum.

Watch Out!

Kids often think that the purpose of the equal sign is to tell them to give an answer. Help your child understand that the equal sign means that the amount on each side of the symbol is the same.

Ask your child to think of a balance scale or to draw one on a piece of paper. Write the equal sign in the middle of the scale, then write a fact such as 6 + 2 on the left side and 8 on the right side. Tell your child that each side must be the same for the scale to balance and for the equal sign to be used. Draw some other scale pictures with examples of the fact and the sum "out of balance." Ask your child, "Can the equal sign be used here?"

What to Know...

Your child uses addition all the time!

Review these skills with your child this way:

- **Addition** is an operation that combines numbers.
- The **sum** is a number that results from adding numbers.
- The **plus sign (+)** is the symbol that tells us to add. The **equal sign (=)** means that the values on each side of it must be equal.

Your child uses addition when painting pictures with a friend.

Ask your child to count how many jars of paint each child has. Then, ask your child to think about how many jars of paint the children would have if they put them together. Ask your child to write this as an addition fact: 3 + 5 = 8.

A bookstore owner needs to add up all of the book orders from customers.

I had 10 book orders this morning and 3 orders this afternoon.

PAID

10 + 3 = 13

Ask your child to connect the owner's words with the number sentence. Then, play shopkeeper with your child. Select several household items and put prices in cents on them. Take turns being the customer and the shopkeeper. The customer selects two items, then takes them to the shopkeeper to add up the total cost. The customer pays in pennies. Remind your child that a penny has the value of one, or one cent.

$$6 + 3 = 9$$
$$3 + 6 = 9$$

Help your child see that it doesn't matter which number you add first; the sum will always be the same. Use the addition fact table on page 174 of this book. Give your child two numbers such as 3 and 6. Have your child use the table to find the sum for 6 + 3 and for 3 + 6. Talk about what happened. Have your kid test this property by giving her other sets of numbers to try.

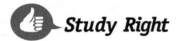 *Study Right*

A fun way to study basic facts is to make a reference book of addition facts with sums your child can feel. Choose a set of addition facts with which your child is having difficulty, such as all the addition facts that include 9. Help your child write one fact without the sum on a piece of paper, such as 9 + 2. Then, have your child illustrate the sum using glitter glue. Once this glue dries, it remains visible and is raised above the paper for your child to feel. If you don't have glitter glue, your child can use fuzzy stickers, or glue on dried beans. Repeat for each fact. Staple the pages together. Now your child can practice the facts by paging through the book and using the illustrations to count and self-check.

First Graders Are...

Children of this age delight in doing what they perceive to be grown-up tasks. They get excited to make symbolic marks like numbers, the plus sign, and the equal sign. It is important to accept and praise their attempts at this type of work, even though their writing skills may not be very neat, their spacing might be off, and some of their numbers might be reversed.

Your child can practice addition with these activities. You'll probably want to read these activities aloud to your child.

On Your Way to an "A" Activities

Type: Active
Materials needed: 11 pieces of paper labeled 0 to 10, masking tape, marker
Number of players: 2

Have "Sum fun!" Put the numbered pieces of construction paper down on a large floor space or in the yard. Hold them down with pieces of tape. Shout, "Jump, grasshopper, jump!" Each player jumps to a number. Together, add the two numbers and say the sum. Keep jumping and adding as long as you can.

Type: Game/Competitive
Materials needed: paper, pencil, deck of cards with face cards removed
Number of players: 2

Each player picks a magic number from 4 to 20. Each player writes his magic number on a piece of paper and places it next to the player on his right. Put the deck of cards facedown in the middle of the play area. Each player takes a card and puts it faceup. Players add the numbers to find the sum. If the sum matches one of the magic numbers, that player collects the cards and wins! Keep playing. The player with the most cards at the end of the game is the winner.

Has your child breezed through the activities? If so, he or she can work on this Using Your Head activity independently. You may want to read the activity below aloud to your child.

Using Your Head

Grab a *pencil*, *markers*, and *paper*!

Draw pictures for the addition facts below. You could draw crackers, blocks, crayons, or pennies. Follow the example.

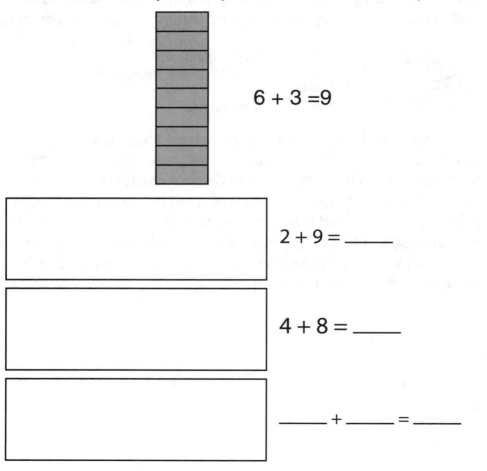

6 + 3 = 9

2 + 9 = _____

4 + 8 = _____

_____ + _____ = _____

Answers: 11, 12, another addition fact

Subtraction

You may have noticed that your child is more comfortable with adding than subtracting. Many kids have an easier time thinking about "putting together" than "taking away." Maybe it's because kids love to get more of something (a few more pieces of candy, five more minutes of playtime before bed), and can't stand to have things taken away (giving one piece of candy away to a sister, taking five minutes away from playtime because of misbehavior).

If your child is quick with addition facts but gets discouraged when you ask for the answer to a subtraction fact, try having her think in terms of addition. For example, with 8 – 3, your child can think "3 and what are 8?" It's important to work with what kids already know. Besides, understanding the relationship between addition and subtraction will carry them much further into the world of mathematics than understanding each in isolation. Of course, it's not enough just to be able to give the answer to any subtraction fact. It's also important for your child to understand that subtraction means groups are getting smaller, in that something has been taken away, and something is left over. Don't forget to connect subtraction to things that are relevant to your child's world.

First things first: Get a sense of what your kid already knows. Turn the page and tell your kid to Jump Right In!

Here's what you'll need for this lesson:
- markers or crayons
- paper
- pennies
- string
- colored beads
- board game
- small household items
- dice

Feel free to read the questions aloud.

 **Jump Right In!**

Use the subtraction facts table below to answer the questions.

–	0	1	2	3	4	5	6	7	8	9	10
0	0	1	2	3	4	5	6	7	8	9	10
1	1	2	3	4	5	6	7	8	9	10	11
2	2	3	4	5	6	7	8	9	10	11	12
3	3	4	5	6	7	8	9	10	11	12	13
4	4	5	6	7	8	9	10	11	12	13	14
5	5	6	7	8	9	10	11	12	13	14	15
6	6	7	8	9	10	11	12	13	14	15	16
7	7	8	9	10	11	12	13	14	15	16	17
8	8	9	10	11	12	13	14	15	16	17	18
9	9	10	11	12	13	14	15	16	17	18	19
10	10	11	12	13	14	15	16	17	18	19	20

1. $3 - 1 =$

   A. 2

   B. 8

   C. 5

   D. 4

2. $15 - 6 =$

   A. 6

   B. 5

   C. 10

   D. 9

3. Choose the subtraction fact that matches the picture.

A. 8 – 2 = 6

B. 2 – 2 = 0

C. 10 – 2 = 8

D. 8 – 0 = 8

4. Draw a picture to show the answer to this subtraction fact:

12 – 6 =

5. Tim ate some strawberries. He had 3 strawberries left. Write a subtraction fact that equals 3.

_____ – _____ = 3

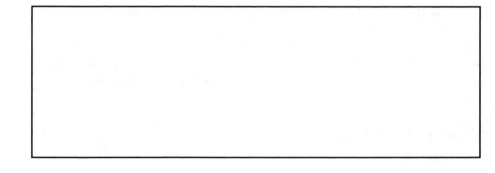

Excellent Job!

 *Checking In*

Ⓐ Answers for pages 182 and 183:

> **1.** A
>
> **2.** D
>
> **3.** A
>
> **4.** An A+ answer: Your child should draw 12 items with 6 items crossed out.
>
> **5.** An A+ answer: A fact with the difference of 3 such as 10 − 7 = 3 or 8 − 5 = 3

Did your child get the correct answers? You could say, "Show me how you used the facts table to get the answers" or "Explain how the picture matches your answer." For question 4, check to see that your child can show you which pictures represent each number in the number sentence.

Did your child get any of the answers wrong? You might want to review using the facts table. First, find the greater number in the body of the table. You will see that the same number shows up several times in the body of the table. You and your child will need to find the smaller number at the very top of the table that shares the same column as the greater number. Circle them both and read the beginning of the fact aloud with your child (3 − 1 =). From the greater number, draw your finger across the row to the left and circle the difference. Say the fact again, this time with the difference (3 − 1 = 2).

Make sure your child understands that the two balloons crossed out in question 3 show balloons that are taken away, or subtracted, from the whole amount.

 *Watch Out!*

Kids may have trouble using the facts table for subtraction. It is important that they understand that the facts table is just one of many tools and strategies that will help them to solve subtraction facts. If your child can solve the facts by crossing out pictures in a drawing, or in her head, that's great. Your child can use whatever feels most comfortable, but don't let that deter you from encouraging her to try out new ideas and strategies. Otherwise your kid will never know which strategy she like the best.

Ask your child to "test" his answers to subtraction facts by using the facts table with another method. For example, have your child solve 13 − 5 on the facts table, then check his answer by drawing a picture or using counters.

What to Know...

Review these skills with your child this way:

- **Subtraction** is an operation on two numbers that tells the difference between the numbers.

- The **difference** is a number that results from subtracting a number from another number.

- The **minus sign (–)** is the symbol that tells us to subtract. The **equal sign (=)** means that the values on each side of it must be equal.

Your child uses subtraction while eating pizza. If the pizza is cut into 8 slices and you and your child eat 3 slices, there are 5 slices left over.

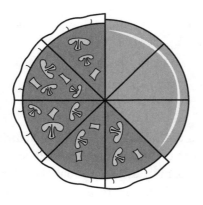

Encourage your child to think about subtraction when you serve pie or cake. Cut the entire pie or cake into pieces. Have your child count the pieces, then serve one piece to each person. Ask your child questions like, "How many pieces did we start with? How many pieces did we serve? What is left in the pan? What is the difference?"

A gardener uses subtraction when planting a vegetable garden.

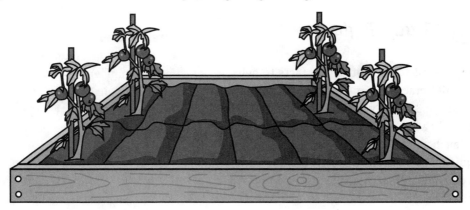

Ask your child to find how many rectangles there are for plants, how many already have plants, and how many rectangles are left to be planted. Ask your child to say the subtraction fact that tells how many rectangles are left to plant ($12 - 4 = 8$).

Your child uses basic subtraction facts when playing games that require counting down by one less, taking one step back, or discarding in a card game.

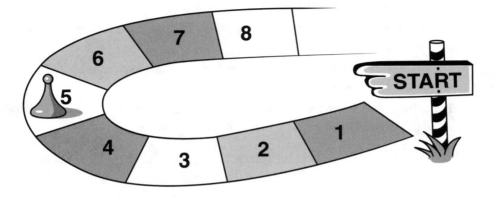

Use the game board to show your child how moving back one space is like the subtraction fact 5 − 1 = 4. Play a board game with your child. Ask your child to say a subtraction (or addition) fact for each move he makes on the board.

 ## Checking In

At this stage, children don't always understand the relationship between addition and subtraction. Games like the one above, as well as tools like the facts table, can help children see the connection. Look for other opportunities to point out the relationship. For example, say, "I moved 5 spaces, but I needed to move 8 to win. 8 − 5 = 3. I need to move 3 more spaces to win. 5 + 3 = 8!"

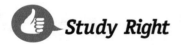 ## Study Right

Use back-and-forth subtraction facts to help your child practice. For example, say a fact, such as 9 − 3. Have your child give the answer as quickly as possible. Next, your child says a fact, such as "10 − 6." Now, you say the answer as quickly as possible. See how quickly you both can go back and forth and still answer all the facts correctly.

First Graders Are...

Kids in this age group are really feeling confident about their speaking skills and love to try them out whenever they get the chance. You may have noticed this "motormouth" quality in your own child. Give your kid something to talk about by encouraging him to explain his mathematical thinking or make up subtraction stories about the facts she is practicing.

Your child can practice subtraction with these activities. You'll probably want to read these activities aloud to your child.

On Your Way to an "A" Activities

Type: Arts and Crafts
Materials needed: a piece of string with one end knotted, colored beads
Number of players: 1 or more

It's time to make some addition and subtraction fact necklaces! String two colors of beads to show a subtraction fact. For example, to show the fact 14 – 4 = 10, your string would have 14 beads total. Ten of the beads would be red and four of the beads would be blue. Say the fact. Separate, or "take away," the 4 blue beads from the 10 red beads to show the difference.

Type: Active
Materials needed: small household items
Number of players: 2 or more

Play Hide-and-Seek Facts! Choose a number of items, such as 10 rubber balls. One player is the hider and the others are the seekers. The seekers count the balls. The seekers close their eyes while the hider puts some balls out of sight, such as three. The seekers open their eyes and use subtraction to tell how many balls are missing (10 – 7 = 3), then find the missing balls.

Using Your Head

{ **20** minutes }

*Grab some **pennies**, a **die**, **paper**, and a **pencil**!*

Use subtraction to play "Path to Zero." Start with 19 pennies and one die. Roll the die and take away that many pennies from the pile. For example, if you rolled a 6, you would then write down "19 – 6 = 13." This is your first step on the "path to zero." Keep rolling, subtracting, and writing each fact until you have zero pennies left in the pile. If you roll a greater number than the number of pennies left in the pile, you must roll again.

Can you make up another game using subtraction, pennies, and a die? Play the game you made up with a family member or a friend.

Number Sentences

Once your child is feeling confident in his or her ability to add and subtract, it is time to push the envelope a little bit. Some equally important skills are knowing *when* to add or subtract and how to write a number sentence. In school, these skills will be learned and practiced by using number stories—which you might remember as word problems.

You may have dreaded word problems when you were in school. You probably recall the standard "If the train is traveling at a rate of 80 miles per hour and takes 3 hours and 20 minutes to get to Chicago..." type of question. If they put a knot in your stomach then, you may worry about how to help your child with word problems and number sentences now. The good news is that your child will use word problems, or number stories, early and often. In fact, the number stories are usually somewhat relatable these days, so your kid might actually be interested in solving them!

Number stories give your child a real-world connection to number sentences. Think of number stories as ways to model, or "act out," addition and subtraction, and number sentences as a numerical way of representing these ideas. As your child masters these skills, he or she will be able to use them interchangeably to solve many mathematical problems, not just in school, but in everyday life.

First things first: Get a sense of what your kid already knows. Turn the page and tell your kid to Jump Right In!

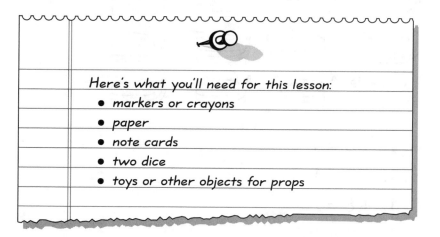

Here's what you'll need for this lesson:
- markers or crayons
- paper
- note cards
- two dice
- toys or other objects for props

Feel free to read the questions aloud.

Jump Right In!

Which number sentence matches the picture?

1.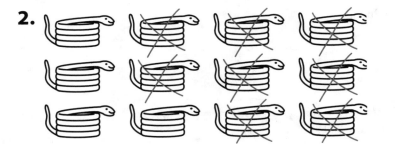

A. $5 + 0 = 5$

B. $5 - 4 = 1$

C. $4 + 5 = 9$

D. $5 + 4 = 9$

2.

A. $12 + 8 = 4$

B. $12 - 8 = 4$

C. $12 + 8 = 20$

D. $12 - 8 = 20$

3.

Sasha put 3 flowers in a vase. There are 5 more flowers on the table. Sasha has 8 flowers in all.

Which number sentence matches the number story?

A. $8 + 3 = 11$

B. $5 - 3 = 2$

C. $8 - 5 = 3$

D. $3 + 5 = 8$

4. Draw a picture that shows this number sentence.

$$7 + 3 = 10$$

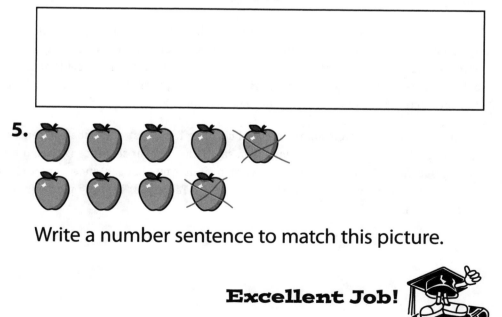

Write a number sentence to match this picture.

Excellent Job!

 *Checking In*

Ⓐ Answers for pages 190 and 191:

1. D
2. B
3. D
4. An A+ answer: Your child should draw seven objects added to three objects to show a total of ten objects altogether.
5. An A+ answer: 9 − 2 = 7

Did your child get the correct answers? You could ask, "How did you know whether to add or subtract?" or "How did you know where the numbers should go?" Make sure your child got the right answer because he knew the skills (and didn't guess).

Did your child get any of the answers wrong? Ask your child to explain her thinking. Read the number story aloud with your child. Help your child identify the key facts. For example, underline the phrases "3 flowers," "5 more," and "8 flowers in all." Point out that the words "more" and "in all" are clues that addition is being used.

 *Watch Out!*

Kids may have a preference for either adding or subtracting. Because of this, they may automatically think of every number sentence as addition or subtraction without looking at the symbols. Remind your child that a plus sign is telling them that two numbers are being added, while the minus sign is telling them that one number is being subtracted, or "taken away," from the other number.

To help your child pay attention to the symbols, give him a list of number sentences. Have him circle the plus or minus sign, then say if the number sentence is telling him to add or subtract. You can also write down two similar number sentences, one addition and one subtraction, such as 6 + 3 = 9 and 6 − 3 = 3. Talk about how the plus sign or minus sign changes the answer.

What to Know...

Your child is learning how to write addition and subtraction number sentences using pictures and number stories, while also determining whether a number story or picture requires addition or subtraction.

Review this skill with your child this way:

- A **number sentence** has an equal sign. The values on both sides of the equal sign are equal. (Your child may call number sentences *number models*.)

Your child could use number sentences to find the total number of stickers.

$$5 + 6 = 11$$

Review the number sentence with your child. Encourage your child to explain the meaning of each number in the number sentence. Challenge your child to think of a situation in which subtraction might be used. Encourage your child to write the number sentence for this situation.

Your child uses number stories and number sentences when playing with a friend.

Encourage your child to make up an addition number story and a subtraction number story and write a number sentence that might describe the picture.

 *Checking In*

If your child is having difficulty translating word problems into number sentences, remind her that a number sentence is just a different way of telling a story using only numbers and symbols. Explain to your child that it is like using another language to say the same thing. For example, in the Spanish language, "my house" is "mi casa." The words sound and look different, but the meaning is exactly the same!

You can also work with a number story in steps to increase your child's understanding. For example, say, "The playground has four swings." Then, have your child draw four swings and write the number 4 below. Next, say, "Over the summer, the town put in two more swings." Your child should draw two more swings and write + 2 below. Point out that since the town put more swings in the playground instead of taking away swings, the plus sign is used to show addition. Finally, say, "Now there are six swings in all." Your child can complete the number sentence by writing = 6.

 *Study Right*

Give your child wide-ruled paper to help her write number sentences properly. Ask her to write all the addition number sentences she can think of for the sum of 10, for example. She can write one number sentence on each line. To practice proper spacing, have your child put one finger after each number or symbol she writes, before writing the next number or symbol. Have her write the plus sign and equal sign in green. Repeat the exercise for subtraction number sentences with the difference of 10, for example. Ask your child to write the minus sign and equal sign in red.

First Graders Are...

Watch your child for a few minutes when he is "pretend" playing. Notice how detailed his scenarios are and how involved he becomes in the imaginative world he has created for himself. Take advantage of this time in his development by encouraging him to create and act out number stories and number sentences.

Your child can practice using and writing number sentences with these activities. You'll probably want to read these activities aloud to your child.

On Your Way to an "A" Activities

Type: Speaking/Listening
Materials needed: note cards, red and green markers
Number of players: 2 or more

Give each player an index card. Label one side of the card with a red minus sign. Flip the card and label this side with a green plus sign. Ask your parent or friend to tell you a number story. For example, "Sunil had five cookies. He gave two to his friend Alyssa. Now Sunil has three cookies left." Hold up the card to show the plus sign if the story uses addition. Hold up the card to show the minus sign if the story uses subtraction. Take turns telling number stories and holding up your card.

Type: Active
Materials needed: toys or objects for props, dice
Number of players: 2 or more

Put on a play! Roll the dice. Use the numbers rolled to create a number story. Act out the number story using toys and objects from your house or yard. For example, if you rolled a 6 and a 1, put six teddy bears to bed, then tuck in one more to make seven teddy bears. See if your audience can say the number sentence you are acting out.

Has your child breezed through the activities? If so, he or she can work on this Using Your Head activity independently. You may want to read the activity below aloud to your child.

Using Your Head

Grab some **markers** or **crayons** and a **pencil**!

Write an addition *or* subtraction number sentence that matches the picture.

_____

Draw a picture for a new word problem, or number story. Write the matching number sentence.

_____

Answer: Either 8 + 6 = 14 or 14 − 6 = 8 can be written. In the case of subtraction, cross out 6 ducks.

'96   Cracking the First Grade

Ways of Representing Numbers

Are you aware that your child is spending time in math composing and decomposing numbers? This might sound a little scary, but it's really not. These terms simply refer to another way of representing numbers using what your child already knows about place value, addition, and number sentences.

Your child has been learning about the place value of digits in numbers, as well as about sets of ones, tens, and hundreds and how they can be regrouped. For example, your kid probably learned that the number 84 has an 8 in the tens place and a 4 in the ones place. She also knows that the 8 stands for 8 tens, or 80, and the 4 stands for 4 ones, or 4. Your kid will learn to decompose the number 84 by using place value: 80 + 4. She will also be able to look at a decomposed number, such as 60 + 5, and compose the number 65.

Remember, most of these ideas are all new to your child. Once your child knows the "building blocks" of the numbers he encounters, he will be more successful at addition and subtraction with larger numbers, and later with multiplication and division concepts.

First things first: Get a sense of what your kid already knows. Turn the page and tell your kid to Jump Right In!

Here's what you'll need for this lesson:
- markers or crayons
- paper
- craft sticks
- note cards
- dimes and pennies
- magazines or newspapers
- scissors
- calculator

Feel free to read the questions aloud.

Jump Right In!

What number is shown?

1. $+$

    A. 40

    B. 47

    C. 70

    D. 74

2. $70 + 9 =$

    A. 9

    B. 70

    C. 79

    D. 709

3. Which shows the number 98 when you break it apart using place value?

A. 9 + 8

B. 900 + 8

C. 80 + 9

D. 90 + 8

4. Write any two-digit number.

_____

Use place value to break apart the number. Write it below.

_____

5. 100 + 70 + 5

Use place value to combine the numbers. Write the number they show.

_____

6. 108

Use place value to break apart the number. Write it below.

_____

Excellent Job!

Checking In

A Answers for pages 198 and 199:

    1. B

    2. C

    3. D

    4. An A+ answer: A number such as 56, then 50 + 6

    5. An A+ answer: 175

    6. An A+ answer: 100 + 8

Did your child get the correct answers? You could ask, "How did you use place value to put the numbers together?" or "What steps do you follow when you break apart a number?" Can your child use place value to break apart the numbers in the other answer choices in question 2?

Did your child get any of the answers wrong? Use a place-value chart to show how to combine numbers. In question 2, ask your child to look at the first number, 70, and tell how many tens make 70. Write the digit 7 in the tens column to show 70. Next, look at the number 9. This number represents how many ones. Write the digit 9 in the ones column.

If your child is having difficulty with breaking apart a number, write the number in a place-value chart. Go over each digit's place. In question 3, nine is in the tens place, which means 9 tens, or 90. Eight is in the ones place, which means 8 ones, or 8. Explain how the plus sign is used to put the value of each digit together to show one number.

Watch Out!

Zero can be a tricky concept for young children. It is important to point out to your child that zero, even though it stands for nothing, is important and necessary.

Write down a few sentences that have meaning for your child and that use numbers with zeroes. For example, you might write, "My daughter's name is Rheya and she is 6 years old. Her birthday is August 20. She weighs 50 pounds. She has 10 dolls in her collection." Read the sentences with your child. Next, rewrite the sentences and omit the zeroes. Now, read them again. Ask your child, "Is this right? What happened when we forgot to include the zeroes in the numbers?"

What to Know...

Your child may learn to use place value to break apart numbers and to put them together.

Your child may learn to break apart numbers by using a diagram.

Review the diagram of the tree to the left with your child. Review the place value for each digit. Practice breaking apart numbers by creating a similar diagram, leaving a blank space at the end of each branch. Have your child fill in the value for each number.

As your child becomes more comfortable counting money, he or she will be putting together or breaking apart numbers using place value.

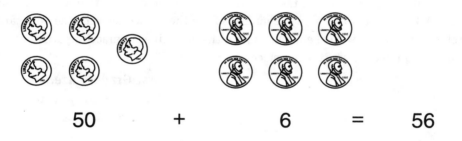

Gather some dimes and pennies. Make groups of varying amounts of coins and have your child combine the numbers to find the total value. If your child is very familiar with money, you might try including dollar bills to use as hundreds.

 *Checking In*

Remember, using place value to break apart numbers is closely related to the concepts of addition and subtraction. When a number is decomposed using place value, an addition fact has been created. Your child can also decompose a number without using place value. For example, give your child 15 craft sticks. Ask her to count the craft sticks and say the number. Now, have your child break apart the number by place value, by grouping the craft sticks by tens or ones. This represents the addition fact 10 + 5. Now ask her to break the number 15 apart by showing any addition fact with the sum of 15, such as eight craft sticks and seven craft sticks. Point out to your child that each shows a different way of representing 15.

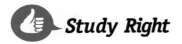 *Study Right*

Ask your child to cut out two- and three-digit numbers from magazines and newspapers. Have him break apart each number using place value and write the numbers on a note card. Shuffle the numbers from the magazines and the note cards, then lay them out on a table. Ask your child to match the numbers from the magazines with the note cards or match the note cards with the numbers from the magazines to practice putting together and breaking numbers apart using place value.

First Graders Are...

First graders are just starting to appreciate a good joke. Remember that there is always room in mathematics for a little stand-up comedy! Make up jokes, limericks, and funny stories using numbers and the concepts your child is practicing. For example, say, "Sixty-seven was so upset, he just fell apart in front of me. His sixty rolled over there and his seven tipped over here!" Who ever thought learning math could be such a riot?

Your child can practice breaking apart and putting together numbers using place value with these activities. You'll probably want to read these activities aloud to your child.

On Your Way to an "A" Activities

Type: Game/Competitive
Materials needed: calculator, lined paper, pencil
Number of players: 2

Punch a two- or three-digit number, such as 99, into the calculator. Give the calculator to your partner. Your partner reads the number and writes it down. Next, your partner is challenged to write the number broken apart by place value: 90 + 9. Check your partner's work by punching 90 + 9 = into the calculator to see if it matches the original number. If it's right, give your partner a point, then switch jobs and play again!

Type: Speaking/Listening
Materials needed: none
Number of players: 2 or more

Every time you say a number, say it broken up by place value. The conversation around your house might sound like this: "Mom, you won't believe this but I have been in school for 40 + 2 days already! Oh, by the way, I need to send Grandma a picture I made. Isn't her house number 100 + 10 + 1?" See how long you can do this. Can you make it until bedtime without forgetting?

Has your child breezed through the activities? If so, he or she can work on this Using Your Head activity independently. You may want to read the activity below aloud to your child.

Using Your Head

{ **10** minutes }

*Grab a **pencil**!*

CODE KEY		
39 = C	83 = K	125 = 0
66 = U	91 = Y	140 = R

Write each number on the line underneath its matching broken-apart number. Use the Code Key to find the matching letters. Write them in the box below each number to see the secret message. Good luck!

90 + 1   100 + 20 + 5   60 + 6

_____   _____   _____

☐   ☐   ☐

100 + 40   100 + 20 + 5   30 + 9   80 + 3

_____   _____   _____   _____

☐   ☐   ☐   ☐ !

Fact Families

Did you use flash cards as a kid? You might have "flash" backs of numbers appearing before your eyes and sweating profusely as you racked your brain for the answer while the timer ticked off the seconds in the background. You may worry that your child is in for the same kind of "fun." Don't worry. Now your kid can use more meaningful tools to learn addition and subtraction facts: fact families and related facts.

Your child might say, "But I already know my facts. Why are we spending more time on them?" This question makes sense. However, if your child knows that $8 - 5 = 3$, then he should also know that $8 - 3 = 5$. When your kid understands fact families, it's like getting *four* facts for the price of one! Using the numbers 3, 5, and 8, your kid should know that $5 + 3 = 8$, $3 + 5 = 8$, $8 - 5 = 3$, and $8 - 3 = 5$!

These concepts are so important for your child to understand and master because they will help him to more clearly see the relationship between addition and subtraction—another step toward building a solid foundation in number sense.

First things first: Get a sense of what your kid already knows. Turn the page and tell your kid to Jump Right In!

Here's what you'll need for this lesson:
- markers or crayons
- paper
- note cards
- dried beans, pennies, or cereal O's
- paper cup
- card stock or cardboard
- scissors
- 3×5 sticky notes
- kitchen timer

Feel free to read the questions aloud.

 **Jump Right In!**

For questions 1 and 2, what is the related addition fact?

1. $4 + 5 = 9$

   A. $9 + 5 = 14$

   B. $9 + 4 = 13$

   C. $5 + 4 = 9$

   D. $4 + 9 = 13$

2. $7 + 4 = 11$

   A. $4 + 7 = 11$

   B. $11 + 4 = 15$

   C. $11 + 7 = 18$

   D. $7 + 11 = 18$

For questions 3 and 4, what is the related subtraction fact?

3. $8 - 2 = 6$

   A. $6 - 2 = 4$

   B. $8 - 6 = 2$

   C. $6 - 4 = 2$

   D. $8 + 2 = 10$

Cracking the First Grade

4. $5 - 1 = 4$

    A. $4 - 1 = 3$

    B. $4 + 1 = 5$

    C. $4 - 3 = 1$

    D. $5 - 4 = 1$

5. Use the numbers 3, 7, and 4 to write a fact family.

    _____

    _____

    _____

    _____

6. Complete the number sentences to show a fact family.

$$8 + 2 = \underline{\hspace{1cm}}$$

$$2 + \underline{\hspace{1cm}} = 10$$

$$10 - \underline{\hspace{1cm}} = 2$$

$$\underline{\hspace{1cm}} - 2 = 8$$

Excellent Job!

 *Checking In*

❶Answers for pages 206 and 207:

    1. C

    2. A

    3. B

    4. D

    5. An A+ answer: $7 - 4 = 3$, $7 - 3 = 4$, $4 + 3 = 7$, $3 + 4 = 7$

    6. An A+ answer: 10, 8, 8, 10

Did your child get the correct answers? You could ask, "Show me how the numbers changed places" or "How do you know a fact is related?" See if your child can explain the "why" behind the concepts. Give your child one number sentence (such as $5 + 4 = 9$) and ask her to write the other three facts to make a fact family.

Did your child get one of the answers wrong? You might ask, "What should you do to find the related fact?" In a related fact and in a fact family, the three numbers used never change, they just switch places. Write three numbers from a fact family on three separate note cards. Label three other note cards with a plus sign, a minus sign, and an equal sign. Start with one fact, such as $7 + 5 = 12$. Have your child rearrange the cards to make the related addition fact. Then, arrange the cards to show $12 + 5 = \underline{\hphantom{xxx}}$. Ask your child, "Is this a related addition fact?" Help your child see that this fact is not related to $7 + 5$ $= 12$ because the sum is 17. Point out that only the numbers being added switch places in related addition facts. Repeat this exercise for related subtraction facts. Show how each time, the subtraction number sentence begins with the largest number, but the number that is being subtracted and the difference switch places.

 *Watch Out!*

Your child might understand related facts easily for addition but not subtraction, or vice versa. Find opportunities to explain one operation by using the other. For example, if your child sees $7 + 8 = 15$, show her how to work backward from the addition fact to find the subtraction fact: $15 - 8 = 7$. You can also ask, "What plus eight equals fifteen?"

What to Know...

Your child is learning how addition and subtraction relate to each other by finding related facts and writing fact families.

Review these skills with your child this way:

- **Related addition facts** are a pair of addition facts that use the same three numbers. (Your child might use the term *turn-around facts*.)

- **Related subtraction facts** are a pair of subtraction facts that use the same three numbers.

- An addition and subtraction **fact family** is a group of two addition facts and two subtraction facts that use the same three numbers.

Fact triangles can help your child practice the basic addition and subtraction facts that make up a fact family.

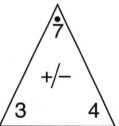

Review a fact family with your child by using the fact triangle. Ask your child to look at the three numbers on the triangle. The number under the dot always indicates the sum, as well as the number to begin with when subtracting. Cover one corner of the fact triangle. Ask your child to give you an addition or subtraction fact that equals the number that is covered. Continue by covering each of the other two numbers. Create other fact triangles with your child. Remember to place the largest number under the dot on each triangle.

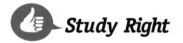 Study Right

If your child is having difficulty with a particular fact family, help him make his own set of fact triangle cards. Cut a square piece of card stock or cardboard diagonally from corner to corner to make two triangles. Have your child label the corners with the numbers in the fact family, marking a dot above the largest number (this indicates the sum, as well as the number to begin with when subtracting), then writing a + and – in the middle. Your child can practice on his own by holding his finger over one of the numbers and finding the sum or difference.

Fact families are useful to know when gathering supplies for a craft project.

How to make a
caterpillar
_____
1 egg carter
8 pipe cleaners
paint

Read the supply list with your child. Look at the items that are gathered in the picture. Ask your child to use what he or she knows about fact families to determine how many more pipe cleaners are needed to make the legs. For example, your child could say, "I can figure out how many more pipe cleaners are needed by $8 - 3 = 5$ or $3 + 5 = 8$. I could also use $8 - 5 = 3$ or $5 + 3 = 8$.

 Checking In

Children at this age still may need a lot of hands-on support with math concepts. Use counters like beans, pennies, or cereal O's to help them get a feel for what they are learning.

Write a fact family down on paper, using the numbers 10, 6, and 4. Model for your child how to show each fact using dried beans and a paper cup. For example, separate the beans into a group of six and four and then a group of four and six, and combine them to show the addition facts. Then, show 10 beans. Put six beans under the cup to show four beans remaining. Reverse to show the other related subtraction fact. Use another fact family and have your child give it a try.

First Graders Are...

Children of this age group are beginning to think abstractly, but they still need to relate what they learn to the concrete world. "Seeing is believing" is a good motto to remember when working with your first grader.

Cracking the First Grade

Your child can practice related facts and fact families with these activities. You'll probably want to read these activities aloud to your child.

On Your Way to an "A" Activities

Type: Arts and Crafts
Materials needed: sticky notes, markers or crayons
Number of players: 1 or more

Make a family album for each fact family. Choose three numbers from a fact family, such as 13, 8, and 5. Remove a section of five sticky notes from the pad, being careful to leave them stuck together. Decorate the first sticky note, the cover, with the numbers you chose. Write each fact in the family, one on each page. Choose one color for each number, such as red for 13, orange for 8, and purple for 5. Draw dots to show a "family picture" above each fact. For example, on the page above $13 - 8 = 5$, draw 13 dots, then cross out eight dots to show five dots left.

Type: Game/Competitive
Materials needed: note cards, markers, kitchen timer
Number of players: 1 or more

Have a parent or friend help you write the addition facts and subtraction facts for eight fact families. Write one fact on each card. You will have 32 note cards in all. Split the pairs of related facts into two groups. Arrange the first group of facts faceup on the table in a 4-by-4 grid. Put the other group of facts facedown in a pile. Draw one card at a time from the pile and make a match with the related fact on the table. Can you match them all in 20 seconds? How about 10 seconds?

Has your child breezed through the activities? If so, he or she can work on this Using Your Head activity independently. You may want to read the activity below aloud to your child.

Using Your Head

Grab a **pencil** and some **crayons**!

Fill in the missing number of each fact triangle. Color any fact triangles that contain the number 11 or 12 yellow. What do you see?

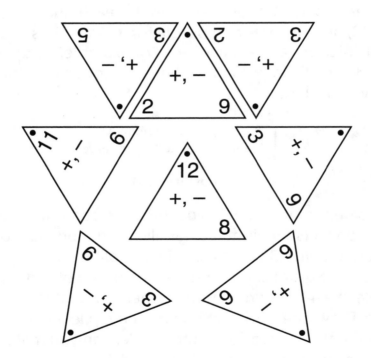

Parts of a Group and of a Whole

Sometimes, it may seem like the math your child is learning now is a completely different animal from the kind of math you did as a kid. You may have read the title of this chapter and thought, "Describing parts of a group and of a whole? What exactly does that mean? And how in the world does it relate to mathematics?"

Describing part of a group of objects or parts of a whole may seem pretty basic to you. For example, in a group of socks, four socks might be red and four might be white. Or a whole pizza might have two pepperoni slices and six plain slices. Counting these parts may seem pretty easy for your child also. However basic it may be, it will to give your child a starting point with fractions. Later on, your kid will learn to represent the part as a numerator and the total or whole as a denominator. Along the way, your child will learn early division concepts as she learns about equal parts of a group or a whole.

First things first: Get a sense of what your kid already knows. Turn the page and tell your kid to Jump Right In!

Here's what you'll need for this lesson:
- *markers or crayons*
- *paper*
- *plastic spoons*
- *colored modeling clay*
- *paper bag*

Feel free to read the questions aloud.

 **Jump Right In!**

What are the parts of each group?

1.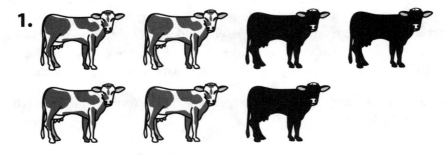

   A. 7 cows
   B. 3 spotted cows, 4 black cows
   C. 4 spotted cows, 3 black cows
   D. 7 spotted cows, 7 black cows

2.

   A. 5 red crayons, 5 gray crayons
   B. 1 gray crayon, 4 red crayons
   C. 1 red crayon, 4 gray crayons
   D. 5 red crayons, 1 gray crayon

Cracking the First Grade

3. What are the parts of the whole?

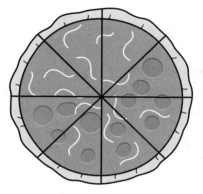

   A. 5 slices with pepperoni, 3 slices plain

   B. 3 slices with pepperoni, 5 slices plain

   C. 8 slices of pizza

   D. 8 slices with pepperoni, 8 slices plain

4. Write the numbers to show the parts of the whole.

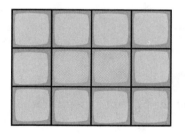

_____ red squares

_____ gray squares

Excellent Job!

 *Checking In*

Answers for pages 214 and 215:

1. C

2. B

3. A

4. An A+ answer: 2 red squares, 10 gray squares

Did your child get the correct answers? You could ask, "How can you tell which is the group and which are the parts?" Listen carefully to your child's explanation to make sure she didn't just take a wild guess. For questions 1 and 2, challenge your child to draw the groups represented in the other answer choices. For question 3, challenge your child to create the pizzas represented in the other answer choices.

Did your child get any of the answers wrong? You might say, "Show me how you found your answer." Remind your child that objects in a group usually have something in common. Look around your home for more examples of parts and groups. Model how to describe these for your child. Say, "The bookshelf has a group of ten books on it. One part is four hardcover books, and one part is six paperback books" or "There are a group of fifteen candies in the candy dish. One part is ten peppermints, one part is three caramels, and one part is two sour balls." See if your child can identify some more examples.

 *Watch Out!*

Your child might wonder why the parts of a group or whole always need to be equal. In math, we want the parts to be equal so we can be sure that we are talking clearly to each other. To help your child understand, give an example. Say you cut a pizza into four parts that aren't equal (some slices are big, some are little). Even if everyone gets one slice, that doesn't mean everyone gets the same amount of pizza because not everyone is getting the same size slice. But if you cut a pizza into four equal parts, then each person gets the same size slice of pizza. When the slices are equal, you can say that each person got one-fourth of the pizza.

What to Know...

Your child is learning about ways to describe groups and wholes by their parts, as well as becoming familiar with "one-half" and "one-fourth."

Review **parts of a group** with your child using the picture below. Point out that there are six balls in the group. The group has two parts. One part has two star balls. The other part has four gray balls.

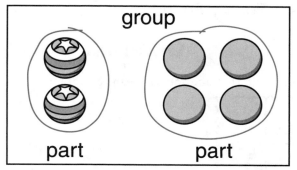

Your child sees parts and groups when getting dressed.

Ask your child to identify the parts of this group of sweaters. Have your child explore her own closet. What can she put into groups? Jackets? Shirts? Pants? How can she describe each part of each group?

Review **parts of a whole** with your child this way:

• A **whole** is a complete thing.

Your child can describe equal parts of a whole.

Ask your child to count the equal parts of this whole. Ask your child to pretend that part of the cake was eaten. Now describe the parts of the whole.

Help your child understand that **one-half** means one of two equal parts:

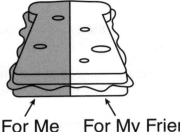

For Me   For My Friend

One-Half

Help your child understand that **one-fourth** means one of four equal parts.

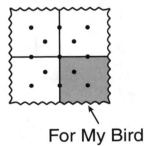

For My Bird

One-Fourth

👉 *Checking In*

There is a subtle, yet crucial difference between the idea of parts of a group and parts of a whole. Your child needs experience with a variety of both types of models for a complete understanding of these concepts. Like for addition and subtraction, children often gravitate toward one type of model over the other.

Encourage your child to use the terms "one-half" and "one-fourth" during meal and snack times. Whip up a part/group and part/whole lunch. See how many different types of models you and your child can make. For example, serve a combination of green grapes and red grapes, or an orange cut into four equal parts!

First Graders Are...

Your child might be anxious to impress you with the quantity of work he can turn out in a sitting. Unfortunately, that means sometimes quality suffers. If you see that your child is rushing through tasks or getting frustrated with spending extended time on activities, it may be time to take a break. Slowing down the pace will help to enhance the quality of his work, while also keeping learning fun for your child.

Cracking the First Grade

Your child can practice describing parts and groups with these activities. You'll probably want to read these activities aloud to your child.

On Your Way to an "A" Activities

{30 minutes} Type: Arts and Crafts
Materials needed: colored modeling clay
Number of players: 1 or more

Have fun making snakes! Use what you know about parts and wholes or parts and groups. For example, roll out four equal pieces of yellow clay and three equal pieces of green clay. Put them together to make a whole snake with four yellow parts and three green parts. You can roll two pieces of red clay into snakes and three pieces of blue clay into snakes to show a group of five snakes with two red parts and three blue parts. You can even make half a snake red and the other half green!

{15 minutes} Type: Game/Competitive
Materials needed: 10 plastic spoons (5 of one color and 5 of another), paper bag, paper, pencil
Number of player: 2

Put the spoons in the bag. Take turns picking out two spoons from the bag without looking. If the spoons you picked show one-half (for example, one clear spoon and one white spoon), you get a point. Players get five turns each. Now, pick four spoons to try to show one-fourth (for example, one clear spoon and three white spoons). Each time you show one-fourth, you get two points. The player with the most points wins!

Has your child breezed through the activities? If so, he or she can work on this Using Your Head activity independently. You may want to read the activity below aloud to your child.

Using Your Head

{ **30** minutes }

*Grab a **pencil** and some **markers** or **crayons**!*

Think of the grid as a whole. Divide the grid into four equal parts. You can use different colors or designs. Describe each part to someone at home.

Comparing and Ordering

Your child already has a ton of experience comparing numbers. Remember how upset your child was when a friend in school received more birthday presents than your child did? Or what about how unfair your kid thought it was that you ate two cookies after dinner and allowed him to eat only one? Without a doubt, your child knows what's more and what's less.

In school, your child will learn fancier words to compare amounts. Instead of using *more, bigger,* or *larger,* your child will learn the term *greater than.* Instead of *smaller,* or *fewer,* your child will learn the term *less than.* Your kid will also learn some new symbols to go with these new terms. Using these new vocabulary words and symbols will certainly make your child sound all grown up, but more importantly, your kid now has another tool to use to see the relationships between numbers.

First things first: Get a sense of what your kid already knows. Turn the page and tell your kid to Jump Right In!

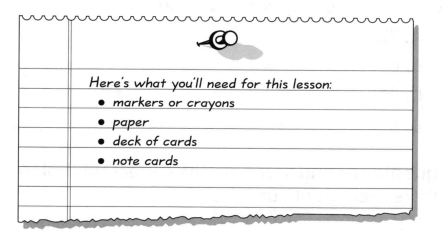

Here's what you'll need for this lesson:
- markers or crayons
- paper
- deck of cards
- note cards

Feel free to read the questions aloud.

Jump Right In!

1. Choose the number that is the greatest.

    A. 2

    B. 9

    C. 5

    D. 4

2. Choose the number that is the least.

    A. 72

    B. 68

    C. 75

    D. 69

For questions 3 and 4, choose the correct symbol to compare each set of numbers.

3. 8 ☐ 6

    A. <

    B. +

    C. >

    D. =

4. 29 ☐ 81

  A. <
  B. +
  C. >
  D. =

5. Write the numbers below in order from least to greatest on the number line.

36, 34, 35

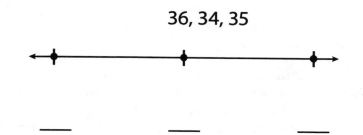

_____   _____   _____

6. Write three numbers in order from greatest to least.

_____, _____, _____

Excellent Job!

Checking In

A Answers for pages 222 and 223:

    1. B

    2. B

    3. C

    4. A

    5. An A+ answer: 34, 35, 36

    6. An A+ answer: A consecutive or nonconsecutive number sequence will be written, such as 78, 77, 76 or 44, 33, 22.

Did your child get the correct answers? You could ask, "Tell me why the number is greater," or "What does that symbol mean?" Make sure your child can explain his or her reason for choosing the answer.

Did your child get any of the answers wrong? For questions 2, 4, and 5, your child might be looking at the greatest digit in a number to determine the answer. It might help to break two-digit numbers into tens and ones to compare them. Help your child write each number in a place-value chart. Start by comparing the number of tens in each number. Point out that in a two-digit number, the number with the most tens is always the greater number. Show your child that when comparing two-digit numbers that have the same amount of tens, you then compare the number of ones to see which number is greater.

Watch Out!

The > and < symbols may be difficult for your child to keep straight. A good way to remember which is which is by thinking of the symbol as a big mouth, like the mouth of a crocodile or a shark, that likes to eat the bigger number. It might even help to cut out a large crocodile mouth. Remember to color both sides of the crocodile to look like the mouth. Tell your child that the crocodile has a big appetite, and so the mouth will always be open to the number that is greater.

What to Know...

Your child compares and orders numbers when he or she wants to know who's older or who has more.

Review these skills with your child this way:

- When you see the symbol >, you can say **"greater than."**
- When you see the symbol <, you can say **"less than."**

Your child might compare quantities of food, such as cookies on a plate, bananas in a bunch, or apples picked.

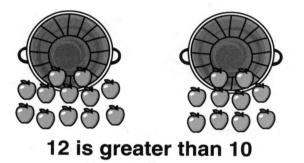

12 is greater than 10
12 > 10

Encourage your child to compare other quantities of food using the terms *greater than* and *less than*. Then, ask your child to write a greater-than or less-than symbol between the numbers to show the comparison.

Your child might compare statistics on a baseball cards.

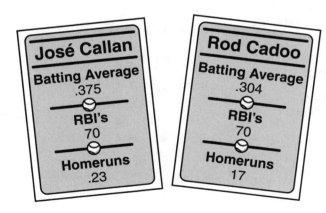

José Callan
Batting Average
.375
RBI's
70
Homeruns
.23

Rod Cadoo
Batting Average
.304
RBI's
70
Homeruns
17

Ask your child to compare the RBI (runs batted in) numbers for each player. Which player's RBI number is greater than the other? Have your child look at the number of home runs. Which player hit fewer home runs than the other? Talk about other examples in sports in which numbers are compared.

Your child may learn to order numbers by using a number line.

Count up the number line to remind your child that each number is one greater than the number before. Count back on the number line to show how each number is one less than the one before. Have your child create a number line with pictures for numbers 1 to 10.

 *Checking In*

Sometimes, children need a visual way to compare numbers. Your child will want to count pictures or items to compare the quantities *and* may also need to match each group up to show a one-to-one correspondence. For example, if your child is trying to determine if she has more markers than crayons, have her line up each group one to one. Model for your child how to make matching pairs of each item until no more matching pairs can be made. The group that has items that don't have a partner is the greater group.

First Graders Are...

Children of this age can be very sensitive and often concerned about making mistakes. Because of this, they are reluctant to take risks when it comes to trying out new concepts or ideas. If your child gets stuck or is having difficulty applying a particular skill, try your best to resist the urge to rush in and "fix" the problem. Instead, encourage your child to try something new. Let your child know that you have confidence in him or her. When helping your child, sometimes less is more!

Your child can practice comparing and ordering numbers with these activities. You'll probably want to read these activities aloud to your child.

On Your Way to an "A" Activities

{15 minutes}
Type: Game/Competitive
Materials needed: deck of cards
Number of players: 2 or more

Remove the Jacks, Queens, and Kings from a deck of playing cards. Shuffle the cards and put them facedown in a pile. Each player takes two cards and adds them to find the sum. The player with the greatest sum takes all of the cards. The player with the greatest number of cards at the end of the game wins! Play the game again, but this time the player with the least sum takes all of the cards.

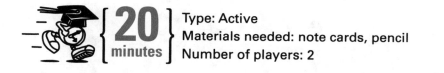

{20 minutes}
Type: Active
Materials needed: note cards, pencil
Number of players: 2

Pick a player to be "less than" and a player to be "greater than." Ask a parent to write several different numbers on note cards. Take turns picking a card and reading the number. "Less than" counts and claps out a number *less than* the number that is on the card. "Greater than" counts and claps out a number that is *greater than* the number on the card.

Has your child breezed through the activities? If so, he or she can work on this Using Your Head activity independently. You may want to read the activity below aloud to your child.

Using Your Head

Grab a **pencil**!

Help the bear find his way through the forest to get to the greatest number of fish.

Put the number of fish shown at each part of the river in order from greatest to least.

——————, ——————, ——————, ——————

Shapes

No doubt shapes have been a part of your child's life for as long as you can remember. Her early mutterings may have included phrases like "red circle" or "purple triangle." Many of her first toys that she played with endlessly encouraged her to fit a shape block through the same-shaped hole. You might think, "My child knows her shapes. I don't need to spend too much time on this."

While your child may not have trouble identifying his shapes, it's now time to dig a little deeper. Does your child know that a square has four sides that are the same length and that a rectangle also has four sides but only the opposite sides are the same length? Does your child understand that a circle has no straight sides, but a triangle has three? Can your child match shapes that are the same shape and the same size? Learning about shapes and their attributes sets the stage for early geometry concepts including manipulating shapes and identifying and constructing three-dimensional shapes.

First things first: Get a sense of what your kid already knows. Turn the page and tell your kid to Jump Right In!

Here's what you'll need for this lesson:
- *markers or crayons*
- *paper*
- *cardboard*
- *household objects*
- *building blocks or pattern blocks*
- *scissors*
- *washable paints*
- *construction paper*
- *plastic plates*
- *magazines*
- *glue*

Feel free to read the questions aloud.

Jump Right In!

Name the shape.

1.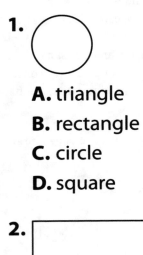

   A. triangle
   B. rectangle
   C. circle
   D. square

2.

   A. triangle
   B. rectangle
   C. circle
   D. square

3. Find the shape that matches.

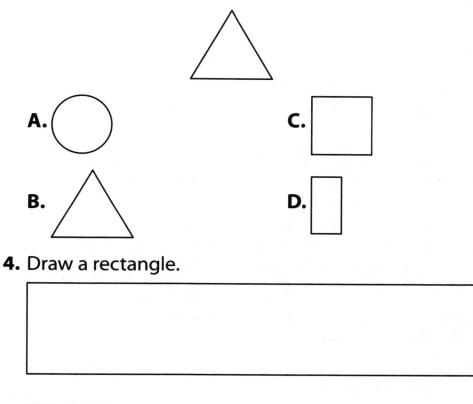

A.

B.

C.

D.

4. Draw a rectangle.

5.

Draw the shape that you would make if you put the two shapes together.

Excellent Job!

Checking In

🅐 Answers for pages 230 and 231:

1. C
2. B
3. B
4. An A+ answer: A rectangle, with opposite sides of equal length, will be drawn.
5. An A+ answer: A square, with four sides of equal length, will be drawn.

Did your child get the correct answers? You could ask, "How do you know that shape is a rectangle?" Be certain that your child understands why he or she chose those answers.

Did your child get any of the answers wrong? You might say, "Tell me why you think those shapes match" or "Describe how you think those shapes fit together." For question 5, if your child is having trouble visualizing the shapes and how they might fit together to make other shapes, use shapes your child can manipulate. For example, cut the same shapes out of cardboard or stiff paper. Let your child put the shapes together and pull them apart to see what happens. Model for your child how to put one shape on top of another to see if they match.

Watch Out!

Many children think a square and a rectangle are the same shape. Draw a distinction by explaining that a square is a special kind of rectangle because all of its sides are the same, or equal, in length. Use examples from around your home to illustrate this point. For example, show your child a square sticky note and a rectangular piece of paper, or a square paper napkin and a rectangular serving platter. Go on a "square and rectangle hunt" with your child, collecting examples of each type of shape.

What to Know...

Your child identifies shapes throughout the day. Your kid might say, "I want to wear my shirt with the blue circles on it." The teacher might ask your kid to sit in a square on the rug.

Review these skills with your child this way:

- A **circle** is a round shape with no straight sides.
- A **triangle** is a shape with three straight sides.
- A **square** is a shape with four square corners and four straight sides. All the sides are the same length.
- A **rectangle** is a shape with four square corners and four straight sides. The opposite sides of a rectangle are the same length.

Use the following picture with your child to review the terms *corner* and *side*:

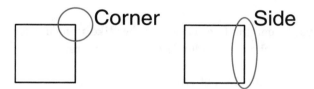

Don't forget your child's artwork! It's made up of all kinds of shapes.

· · · · · · · · · · · · · ·

Ask your child to identify each shape used in the picture. Encourage your child to describe the attributes as well (number of sides and number of corners).

Your child matches, separates, and combines shapes when building with blocks or building models.

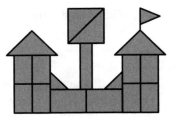

Help your child compare the shapes in the picture. Ask your child, "Are there any shapes that can be made by putting together two other shapes? Are there any that can be made by taking a shape apart?" Use construction paper shapes to experiment with these ideas.

 *Checking In*

Your child may just be getting familiar with terms like *straight sides* and *square corners*. Give your kid plenty of chances to identify these attributes.

Sort shapes with your child. Cut out circles, squares, rectangles, and triangles from construction paper. Ask your child to perform several kinds of sorts on the group. For example, your kid can sort them by number of sides, square corners versus nonsquare corners (such as the corners on triangles), size, texture, or color.

First Graders Are...

At this age, your child's ability to formulate ideas may outpace her ability to express herself on paper. While her fine motor skills and hand strength are both developing rapidly, it may not be fast enough to head off frustration when trying to draw a straight line or a sharp corner. Materials like rubber stamps, stickers, precut paper shapes, cookie cutters, and stencils will give your child the freedom to create, explore, and express without disappointment.

Your child can practice working with shapes with these activities. You'll probably want to read these activities aloud to your child.

On Your Way to an "A" Activities

30 minutes

Type: Arts and Crafts
Materials needed: washable paint, construction paper, plastic plates
Number of players: 2 or more

Wear an old shirt or smock. Put some paint on a plastic plate. Find different-shaped objects around your house that can be used as stamps. Dip the object in the paint and stamp it on paper. Some examples include a cut cucumber or potato, the bottom of a box, or the bottom of a cheese triangle. When your painting is dry, write the name of each shape you made.

20 minutes

Type: Active
Materials needed: paper, pencil
Number of players: 2 or more

Have a shape scavenger hunt. Compete with a friend to find the greatest number of circles, triangles, squares, and rectangles in your home in under 15 minutes. When you find a shape, draw it on your paper and label it. For example, draw a picture of a clock, and label it *circle*. When 15 minutes is up, compare papers. Whoever found the most shapes wins!

 *Study Right*

Help your child make a book of shapes. Staple several pieces of paper together. At the top of each page write the name of a shape. Ask your child to search through an old magazine to find examples of that shape. Cut out the example and glue it on the page. Your child can reference this shape book anytime!

Has your child breezed through the activities? If so, he or she can work on this Using Your Head activity independently. You may want to read the activity below aloud to your child.

Using Your Head

Grab some *markers* or *crayons*!

Find as many circles, triangles, squares, and rectangles as you can. Look carefully! Some shapes have smaller shapes hidden inside of them.

Color circles in blue, triangles in yellow, squares in red, and rectangles in green.

Slides, Flips, and Turns

The title of this chapter might lead you to believe that you are about to leave the world of mathematics and start reading about extreme sports, but that is not the case! These terms describe how your child is learning to identify and visualize two-dimensional shapes as they move through space. In other words, what happens to a square when it slides across the page? What does a triangle look like when it is flipped over? Is a rectangle still a rectangle when it is turned? These are the types of questions your child is exploring.

To you, the answers to these questions seem obvious; however, your child is just beginning to notice and process these types of details. At this point, your child may have a specific "picture" in his head of what a triangle looks like, for example. He knows it has three sides, but in his mind, it might also be large, equilateral, and pointed straight up. Your child is learning that while all triangles have three sides, they can be different sizes, can be oriented in different ways, and can look different from one another.

Your child's ability to plan and anticipate visually and spatially is just beginning to develop. When your child draws, manipulates, and reorients these shapes using flips, slides, and turns, he is building and enhancing his understanding of spatial relations.

First things first: Get a sense of what your kid already knows. Turn the page and tell your kid to Jump Right In!

Here's what you'll need for this lesson:
- *markers or crayons*
- *paper*
- *cardboard*
- *household objects*
- *glue*
- *scissors*
- *books*
- *square paper*
- *napkins and plate*
- *items for collage*
- *tape*

Feel free to read the questions aloud.

Jump Right In!

1. Which picture shows a slide?

A.

B.

C.

D.

2. Which picture shows a triangle flipped?

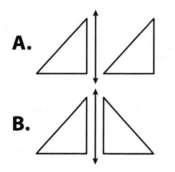

A.

B.

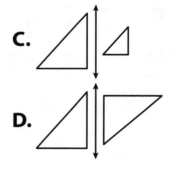

C.

D.

3. Which picture shows a square turned?

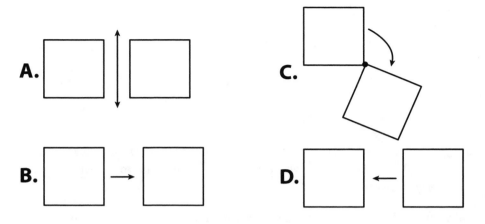

A.

B.

C.

D.

4. Draw this shape flipped over the line.

5. Draw this shape turned.

Excellent Job!

 *Checking In*

⦿ Answers for pages 238 and 239:

    1. D

    2. B

    3. C

    4. An A+ answer: An upside-down heart, flipped over the line

    5. An A+ answer: A triangle, turned slightly around one of its points

Did your child get the correct answers? You could ask, "How did you know what the shape would look like when it was flipped?" Ask your child to tell why the other answers wouldn't work.

Did your child get any of the answers wrong? You might say, "What do you think it means to *turn* a shape?" or "Explain how you would move the shape." The best way to help your child visualize each movement is to give him or her actual shapes to use. Cut some shapes out of paper. Have your child work through each problem while manipulating each shape, then describe what happened.

 *Watch Out!*

Children can get easily confused by the terms *slide, flip,* and *turn.* Give them novel ways to remember each. For example, if your child likes to dance, you might have her think of the terms *slide, flip,* and *turn* as she performs a dance called "The Electric *Slide*." Have your child *slide* to the left or right, do a tumbling *flip,* and *turn* around in circles.

What to Know...

Flips, slides, and turns are ways of moving or transforming two-dimensional shapes.

Review these skills with your child this way:

- To **slide** a shape means to move it along a straight line.

Your child might slide a plate across the table or a toy car across the floor. Sit across the table from your child. Slide an object across to him or her. Say "slide" as you do this. Ask questions like, "Does the plate/toy car look the same?" and "What changed?"

- To **flip** a shape means to move it over a line.

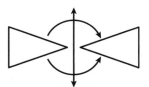

Your child has experienced a flip when he or she has flipped a book over or flipped a flat rock to look underneath it.

Gather some books. Arrange them on one side of the seam of a table or make a line using string. Ask your child to look at the front covers of the books. Now, have your child flip the books over the seam or line. What does he notice? Point out that the books were flipped over from the front side to the back, which explains why all the back covers of the books are visible now. Experiment with other shapes in this way.

- To **turn** a shape means to move it around a point.

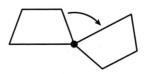

Your child has turned a photograph to show a friend or family member or has watched you turn a road map to get a better view.

Sit next to your child at a table. Place a photograph or road map on the table in front of you. Ask your child to turn the photograph or road map toward her so that she can see it. Model for your child how when turning the shape, one point of the shape stays in the same place while the others move. Have your child keep one point stationary while moving the photo or turning the map in different directions. Try this out with other objects.

Checking In

Your child might notice that the circle can sometimes be the odd one out when it comes to some of these transformations. Have your child flip, slide, and turn something circular, like a plate. Talk about why the circle looks the same when you flip it and turn it. Discuss how the circle has no straight sides or points and how this might affect each transformation.

Study Right

Give your child cardboard cutouts or blocks in the shapes of triangles, circles, squares, and rectangles. Have your kid practice slides, flips, and turns by tracing each shape, making the movement, then tracing it again. Help your child to label each picture. Hang this up near your child's work area for easy and quick reference.

Your child can practice working with slides, flips, and turns with these activities. You'll probably want to read these activities aloud to your child.

On Your Way to an "A" Activities

30 minutes

Type: Arts and Crafts
Materials needed: 2 pieces of cardboard, tape, items for collage, glue
Number of players: 1 or more

Make a collage you will flip for! Collect shapes from around the house or yard. Some ideas are leaves, buttons, flower petals, different kinds and sizes of paper, stickers, or pictures cut from magazines. You must get two of each kind of shape. Tape the cardboard pieces together along the edge. Make a collage with one set of shapes by gluing them onto the left piece of cardboard. Now, show what those shapes would look like flipped over the taped edge by gluing the other set of shapes onto the cardboard piece on the right.

10 minutes

Type: Active
Materials needed: square paper napkins, masking tape, die
Number of players: 2 or more

Can you get from here to there? Find a start point and a finish point on a large area, like a floor or table. Mark the start and finish with a small piece of tape. Each player puts a napkin at the start. Players take turns rolling the die and moving. If the player rolls a 1 or 2, he slides his napkin. If a player rolls a 3 or 4, he flips his napkin. If a player rolls a 5 or 6, he turns his napkin. If one slide gets a player to the finish line, the distance from start to finish is not long enough. The first player to get to the finish line wins!

First Graders Are...

Many children in this age group are driven by a curiosity about how things work. Machines, robots, complicated crafts, and interlocking blocks are favorite toys. Playing with these toys is a great way for your child to put geometry and spatial relations into action. Remember, play remains a powerful tool for learning.

Has your child breezed through the activities? If so, he or she can work on this Using Your Head activity independently. You may want to read the activity below aloud to your child.

Using Your Head

[20] minutes

*Grab a **pencil** and **crayons** or **markers**!*

Look at the puzzle pieces. Imagine how you could fit them into the puzzle using slides, flips, and turns. Write what you did next to each.

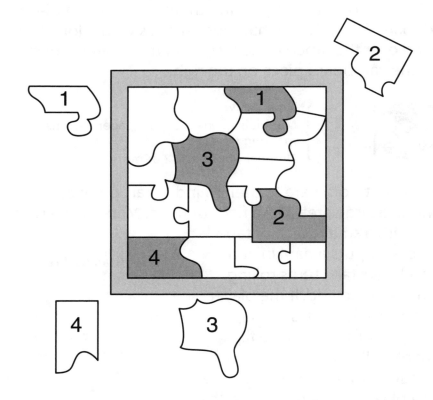

Answers: 1. slide; 2. turn; 3. slide; 4. turn

Patterns with Shapes

Most children love patterns. Kids love to doodle them on the edge of their drawings. They love to wear clothes with colorful patterns. They notice them in Grandma's curtains or on the tablecloth in their friend's house. By first grade, children are beginning to understand that patterns exist everywhere—in nature, at home, at school, in objects, pictures, designs, and even numbers.

Discovering, identifying, and describing patterns is exciting for your child. However, children's natural curiosity and impatience to get to the bottom of things sometimes get in their way. Many times, kids try to identify patterns without "reading" them fully or by overgeneralizing shapes, which causes them to miss the small details, like the size or placement of the shapes. Help your child learn to slow down—details are important! Learning how to find, identify, and continue patterns are skills that will help your kid solve problems in mathematics now and for years to come.

First things first: Get a sense of what your kid already knows. Turn the page and tell your kid to Jump Right In!

Here's what you'll need for this lesson:
- *black marker*
- *crayons*
- *paper*
- *small household objects*
- *box*

Feel free to read the questions aloud.

Jump Right In!

1. Which picture shows a pattern?

A. ○ □ △ ▭

C. △ □ △ □ △ □

B. ♡ ☆ ◇

D.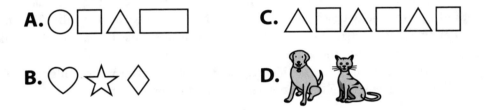

2. What shape comes next in the pattern?

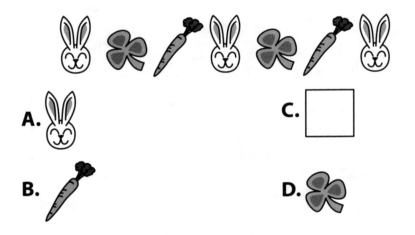

A.

C.

B.

D.

3. What is the rule in this pattern?

○□□○□□○□□○

- **A.** 1 circle, 1 square
- **B.** 2 circles, 1 square
- **C.** 1 circle, 2 squares
- **D.** 2 circles, 2 squares

4. Show a pattern using two shapes.

5. Continue the pattern.

△ ☆ ♡ △ ☆ ♡

Excellent Job!

 *Checking In*

A Answers for pages 246 and 247:

1. C
2. D
3. C
4. An A+ answer: A repeated pattern using any two shapes will be drawn (circle, square, circle, square).
5. An A+ answer: A triangle, star, and heart will be drawn.

Did your child get the correct answers? You could ask, "How can you tell when the shapes show a pattern?" or "How do you know which shape comes next?" Challenge your child to turn the other answer choices for question 1 into a pattern.

Did your child get any of the answers wrong? You might ask, "Which part of the pattern is repeated?" or "Tell me why you chose that shape next." Help your child identify the repeated part of the pattern by circling each segment that repeats. Say the order of the shapes aloud in each repeated part.

 *Watch Out!*

Kids who are more comfortable learning in different ways, such as by listening or by manipulating objects, might have difficulty because patterns printed on a page suit the visual-spatial learner best.

It helps to represent these patterns in different modes to reach all types of learners. For example, saying each shape in the pattern aloud allows the auditory learner to "hear" the pattern, while laying out the pattern using blocks or cut-out shapes is a great way to reach a "hands-on" learner.

What to Know...

Patterns aren't found only in math class; they're in nature as well. Think about the patterns found on butterflies, bees, and zebras.

Review these skills with your child this way:

- A **pattern** is a series of numbers, figures, or pictures that follows a rule.
- A **rule** is a statement that tells how the items in a pattern are related.

Your child might describe and identify patterns around the house.

Ask your child, "Describe the pattern around the edge of the rug. What shapes are repeating?" Ask your child to look at the rugs, drapes, floors, and bedspreads around your home for patterns.

Your child can find the rule for a pattern on her coat, backpack, hair band, or school folder.

Ask your child to describe the pattern on the coat and backpack, and explain the rule for each pattern. Find objects around your home to use to make patterns, such as buttons and pencils, or stickers, rubber stamps, and beads. Ask your child to create patterns and explain each rule.

Your child might predict what comes next in a pattern when setting the table or helping you decorate for a birthday party.

Ask your child to look for a pattern in the place settings and explain the rule (fork, plate, knife). Look for other opportunities in which your child can finish patterns, like when arranging food on a platter, decorating a cake, or sorting socks from the laundry.

 *Checking In*

All this work with patterns may have awakened the pattern "beast" in your child. Your child might be noticing all kinds of patterns now, not just the ones you've been working with in this lesson. For example, he or she might have discovered growing patterns, which are patterns that increase by the same amount each time, such as one red square, two blue squares, three green squares, and so on. Don't dissuade your kid from exploring these new patterns. Instead, ask him or her to compare different types of patterns.

First Graders Are...

Kids at this age often maintain a vise-like grip on their pencil. This often causes their written work to be expressed using tense, tiny letters, numbers, and shapes. Give your child a hand at loosening up by providing her with tools that help her writing and drawing flow, like fat pencils or markers and smooth crayons.

Your child can practice working with patterns with shapes with these activities. You'll probably want to read these activities aloud to your child.

On Your Way to an "A" Activities

{ **20** minutes }

Type: Active
Materials needed: box, groups of assorted objects
Number of players: 2 or more

Have fun with a pattern box! Search around your house and yard for groups of objects you can use to make patterns. For example, lengths of yarn, marbles, coins, crayons, shells, and paper cups can all be used to make patterns. Put them all in the box. Create a pattern on the floor using the objects. Keep the remaining objects in the box. Ask the other player to explain the rule and continue the pattern. Then, switch roles!

{ **30** minutes }

Type: Arts and Crafts
Materials needed: paper, crayons, black marker
Number of players: independent

You can make a pattern with your name! Ask someone to help you make a grid on paper with 10 rows and 8 columns. Use a black marker to print your name, putting one letter for each box. No squares can be left empty. If you can't fit your entire name on one row, go ahead and write the rest of it on the next row, then repeat until all the boxes are filled. Then, fill in each letter box with a different color. For example, blue for boxes with the letter A, red for boxes with the letter D, and so on. Once you are finished, you will see some patterns! Can you describe these patterns to someone?

Has your child breezed through the activities? If so, he or she can work on this Using Your Head activity independently. You may want to read the activity below aloud to your child.

Using Your Head

[**15** minutes]

*Grab a **pencil** and some **crayons** or **markers**!*

Finish the patterns. Add your own patterns in the blank spaces.

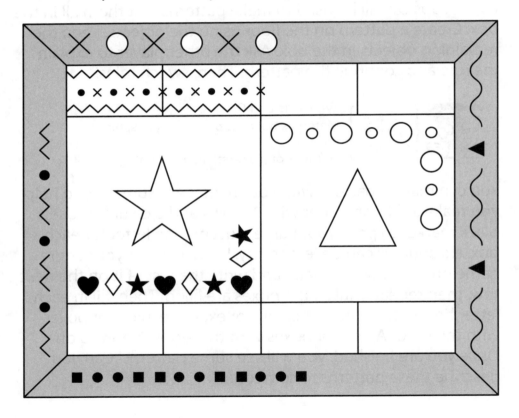

Patterns with Numbers

While your child might easily see and create patterns with shapes, patterns with numbers may prove to be a bit more challenging. For a child who is just becoming "automatic" with counting by ones to numbers like 100 and beyond, looking at a series of seemingly unrelated numbers might be a daunting task. However, your child might be more familiar with number patterns than you realize. If your child plays sports, he or she might have participated in a team cheer after the game. Do you remember hearing, "Two, four, six, eight, who do we appreciate?"

Your child might be more familiar with the term *skip counting* than *number patterns*. Children are taught to look at a number line and *skip* numbers as they count. At first, they learn that skip counting can be used when you want to count something quickly. It's much faster to count the kids in a class by 2s than by 1s. Later on, skip counting will be the foundation for multiplication and division concepts, as well as algebra concepts.

First things first: Get a sense of what your kid already knows. Turn the page and tell your kid to Jump Right In!

Here's what you'll need for this lesson:
- *markers or crayons*
- *paper*
- *small items to use for counting*
- *note cards*

Feel free to read the questions aloud.

 **Jump Right In!**

1. Which shows counting by 2s?

   A. 1, 2, 3, 4, 5, 6

   B. 2, 3, 4, 5, 6, 7

   C. 5, 10, 15, 20, 25

   D. 2, 4, 6, 8, 10

2. What number comes next in the pattern?
10, 20, 30, 40, ☐

   A. 10

   B. 41

   C. 50

   D. 100

3. What is the rule in this pattern?
30, 25, 20, 15, 10, 5

   A. + 5

   B. – 5

   C. + 10

   D. – 10

4. Write the number pattern that matches the dots in the picture.

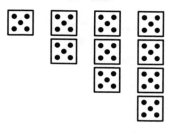

_____, _____, _____, _____

5. Continue the pattern.

40, 50, 60, 70, 80, _____, _____

6. Show a number pattern that uses the rule + 2.

_____, _____, _____, _____

Excellent Job!

Checking In

Ⓐ Answers for pages 254 and 255:

    1. D

    2. C

    3. B

    4. An A+ answer: 5, 10, 15, 20

    5. An A+ answer: 90, 100

    6. An A+ answer: A series of numbers that increase by 2, such as: 10, 12, 14, 16

Did your child get the correct answers? If so, check to make sure your child knows basic number patterns by asking him or her to count by 2s, 5s, and 10s.

Did your child get any of the answers wrong? If so, you might ask, "How did you figure out the rule for the numbers used?" or "Why did you choose that number to come next in the pattern?" Encourage your child to look for clues in the series of numbers—for example, the numbers end in zero, or the numbers are increasing instead of decreasing. These clues will help your kid determine the rule. Once your child has found the rule, have him or her apply the rule to each number in the series to check the answer.

Watch Out!

Kids with different learning styles might need number patterns represented in different ways. Tell your child to say the number aloud to hear the pattern, or have your child make groups of X's or stacks of pennies for each number to see how the numbers change within the sequence. Use other tools, such as a number line or a hundred chart (a 10-by-10 grid that lists numbers 1–100 from left to right, starting at the top left corner) to help your child explore, investigate, and identify how a series of numbers is arranged.

What to Know...

Learning to describe, identify, predict, and create patterns with numbers helps your child understand number relationships.

Your child might notice patterns with numbers at the baseball stadium or school auditorium.

Ask your child, "Which number patterns are used to organize the field boxes and the rows? What are the rules?" Can your child think of any other examples where number patterns are used to organize areas or objects?

Your child might find the rule in a pattern and then predict the next number.

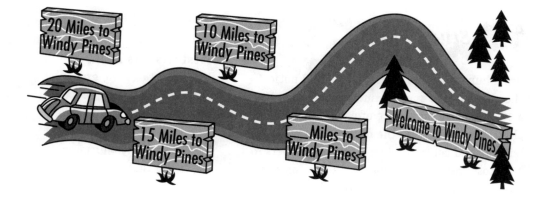

Ask your child what number should be on the fourth road sign, and to define the rule for this pattern. Help your child apply the rule to test her answer. Look for more patterns, such as with the car speedometer, the oven temperature dial, a thermometer, or the bathroom scale.

Checking In

Children may become confused between the pattern's rule and the digits in each number pattern. For example, a child may think that a number pattern that uses the rule + 2 must have a 2 in one of its digits, or that when counting by 5s each number should have a 5 in the ones place.

Have your child pretend to use a "number generator machine" to understand how the numbers in a pattern are determined. Write the rule for a pattern, such as + 2, on a piece of paper. Put the paper on the table. Explain to your child how the number generator machine works: First, put two counters at the top of the paper. Ask your child to imagine putting the two counters through the machine with the rule of + 2. (You can place the two counters underneath the paper to pretend that the machine is working.) Ask your child, "What number would come out the other end?" Put four counters at the bottom of the piece of paper to illustrate the rule. Give your child other numbers to put through the "machine." Have your kid write down the number pattern that the "machine" generated.

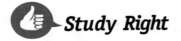

Study Right

Use a hundred chart to help your child notice the attributes of specific number patterns. Make a 10-by-10 grid on a piece of paper. Have your child start by writing the number 1 in the upper left box and continuing writing the numbers to 10 across the first row. Your child can continue writing numbers in this way, from left to right, until the chart is filled and number 100 appears in the box at the lower right. Next, have your child use crayons to color in different patterns. Look at the numbers in each pattern with your child. Talk about which digits are repeated and which numbers are shared by each counting pattern.

First Graders Are...

Your once talkative, exuberant chatterbox may now be developing into a more quiet, determined, and serious student. While previously blurting out every idea that crossed his or her mind, your child may now prefer a quiet area or some alone time to work through concepts and skills, before sharing his or her thoughts with you. If possible, provide your child with a special space for relaxing, thinking, and trying out new concepts. Make this area quiet and comfortable and stock it with art supplies, paper, pencils, a calculator, small objects to count, and other materials.

Cracking the First Grade

Your child can practice working with patterns with numbers with these activities. You'll probably want to read these activities aloud to your child.

On Your Way to an "A" Activities

20 minutes

Type: Active
Materials needed: none
Number of players: 4 or more

Gather a group of friends or family members. Line them up and look for number patterns. For example, each person has two legs, so four people have two, four, six, eight legs! What other number patterns can you find? Hint: Look at clothing and other body parts too. Say the number patterns together. Name the rule for each pattern.

15 minutes

Type: Game/Competitive
Materials needed: note cards, pencil
Number of players: 3

Use note cards to make three sets of counting pattern cards. For example, write the pattern for counting by 2s to 30 on one set of cards, the pattern for counting by 5s to 30 on the second set of cards, and the pattern for counting by 10s to 100 on the third set of cards. Shuffle each set of cards, and keep them separate. Each player gets a set of cards and tries to unscramble the number pattern as quickly as possible. The player who arranges the pattern correctly first wins. Play again!

Has your child breezed through the activities? If so, he or she can work on this Using Your Head activity independently. You'll probably want to read the activity below aloud to your child.

Using Your Head

{ 20 minutes }

*Grab a **pencil** and **crayons** or **markers**!*

Something is missing! Find the rule for the number pattern shown by each picture. Complete the picture to show what is missing. Write the number pattern below.

_____ , _____ , _____ , _____

Tell someone at home a story using the pictures and the number patterns.

Answers: 9 doughnuts are drawn; 3, 6, 9, 12

Measuring Length

At first glance, measuring length appears to be a fairly easy and straightforward skill to learn. Your child might already know the procedure involved with measuring length: Line up the ruler next to the object being measured, then read the number. However, does your child know what it *means* to measure length? Does he or she understand why the object and the ruler need to be lined up correctly? Can your kid grasp why nonstandard units of measurement such as paper clips or straws cannot overlap? If your kid is using different-sized units to measure the length of the same object, can he or she predict how the difference in size of the units will affect the final measurement? When your child can understand and answer these types of questions, you will know that he or she is learning the concepts of measuring length, and not just the procedure.

You might be thinking, "What exactly are nonstandard units and why use them? Why not just stick with standard measuring units such as inches, feet, and yards?" Using a combination of nonstandard and standard units when measuring length puts the focus on the attribute of length, not on the unit itself. The objective here is to help your child learn about length and how it is measured, not specifically to define an inch or a foot. Also, using nonstandard units to measure length is a good way to open up a discussion about why standard units are important and necessary when we measure, compare, and communicate ideas about length. Like every good mathematician, your child will not only understand the *how* of these concepts, but he or she will also know the *why*.

First things first: Get a sense of what your kid already knows. Turn the page and tell your kid to Jump Right In!

Here's what you'll need for this lesson:
- markers or crayons
- paper
- ruler, tape measure, and yardstick
- household objects
- scissors
- string

Feel free to read the questions aloud.

Jump Right In!

1. How long is the edge of the paper?

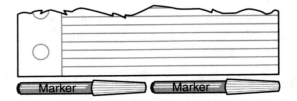

A. 3 markers

B. 2 markers

C. 1 marker

D. 0 markers

2. How long is the pencil?

A. 1 paper clip

B. 2 paper clips

C. 3 paper clips

D. 4 paper clips

Cracking the First Grade

3. How long is the backpack?

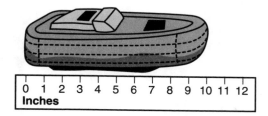

A. 12 inches

B. 10 inches

C. 10 backpacks

D. 8 inches

4. Use a ruler to measure the length of the red edge of this school picture using inches. Write the number and the unit.

_____

Excellent Job!

 *Checking In*

A Answers for pages 262 and 263:

   1. B
   2. C
   3. B
   4. An A+ answer: 2 inches

Did your child get the correct answers? If so, you could say, "Tell me how you found the length." Ask your child to explain how he or she matched the length of the object to the number of units. Check to see that your child can show you the inch side of a ruler and the centimeter side of a ruler.

Did your child get any of the answers wrong? If so, you might ask your child to show how he or she used the ruler to measure the picture. Model for your child the importance of carefully matching the units of measurement being used with the length of the object being measured. Demonstrate how to line up the zero end of the ruler with the edge of the object being measured.

 *Watch Out!*

When measuring length, children may think they are just using a tool to find a number. Help your kid focus on the concept rather than the procedure. Remind your child that he or she is matching the length of one object to another and essentially comparing them.

It is helpful to discuss comparisons before actually measuring the object. For example, when asking your child to measure the length of a pencil using nonstandard units, ask, "What would be better to use, paper clips or straws?" Talk about how each unit compares to the pencil, and make estimates. For example, you might say, "The straw looks about as long as the pencil. The paper clips are much shorter than the pencil. I will guess that the pencil is about three paper clips long."

What to Know...

Measuring length uses many math skills your child has been learning and practicing, such as reading, writing, and comparing numbers, as well as estimating, counting, and geometry.

Review this skill with your child this way:

- **Length** is a measure of the distance between two points.

Your child probably measures length using nonstandard units all the time during play. He or she might measure the length of worms found in puddles with his or her shoe.

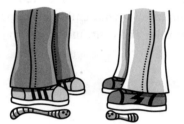

Ask your child to use his or her shoe to measure the length of other objects, such as the kitchen table, the doormat, or the family cat.

 *Checking In*

Have your child repeat the measurements using one of *your* shoes. Ask, "Why are the measurements different?" Talk about why standard units of measure, like feet and inches, make sense.

Your child might get measured at the doctor's office. Standard units like inches and feet are used to measure the height of your kid.

Discuss different types of length measurements, such as height, width, depth, and distance, with your child. Try to find examples of each around your home. Use rulers or tape measures to find length measurements of each example.

Checking In

Now that your child is becoming familiar with the concept of length, he or she should get a lot of practice with measurement tools. Children often make mistakes when using rulers. They may have difficulty lining up the ruler, or they may hold the ruler awkwardly. They can also lose their place if they need to find the length of an object that is longer than the ruler itself.

You may wish to mark the zero end of the ruler with a sticker or dot to help your child remember where to line up the object she is measuring. Model the "problems" of measuring length and how to get around them. For example, if you are measuring something that is longer than the ruler, demonstrate for your child how to put your finger down at the ruler's end, then realign the ruler and continue measuring the length of the object.

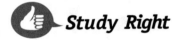

Study Right

Your child should have a pretty good sense of the length of one inch. To help your child with this, create an inch book. Find several objects around your house that are one inch long. Your child can draw pictures of these objects to scale in his or her book. Whenever your child needs to be reminded about the length of an inch, he or she will have this book full of familiar objects to refresh his or her memory.

First Graders Are...

Children in this age group enjoy puzzles, mysteries, clues, secret codes, and "spy" games. Learning can often be more fun when packaged using these themes. For example, give your child a series of length measurements to measure a "pathway" to an object hidden in a room, or tell your child you are thinking of a mystery object that is six inches in length. Have your child measure objects to try to identify the mystery object.

Your child can practice working with measuring length with these activities. You'll probably want to read these activities aloud to your child.

On Your Way to an "A" Activities

Type: Active
Materials needed: string, scissors, yardsticks
Number of players: 2 or more

Try measuring the length of curves! Put a piece of string around your waist. Cut the string when it meets the other end. Pull the string straight and lay it on the floor or table. Measure its length using the yardstick. Do the same to measure the length around the top of your head, your upper arm, or your ankle. Compare the lengths you measured with a friend's or parent's results.

Type: Game/Competitive
Materials needed: nonstandard measuring units, ruler, objects with length
Number of players: 2 or more

Choose a nonstandard unit of measure, such as paper clips, or a standard unit of measure, such as inches. Each player estimates the length of an object, such as a soup spoon, in the chosen units. Now, work together to measure the object's length. The player whose guess was the closest to the actual length measurement wins. Choose another object and unit of measure and play again!

Has your child breezed through the activities? If so, he or she can work on this Using Your Head activity independently. You may want to read the activity below aloud to your child.

Using Your Head

{ **20** minutes }

Grab a **pencil** and a **ruler**!

Which inchworm has the shortest path to the leaf? Measure the length of each path in inches. Write the number sentence to add the measurements together to find out.

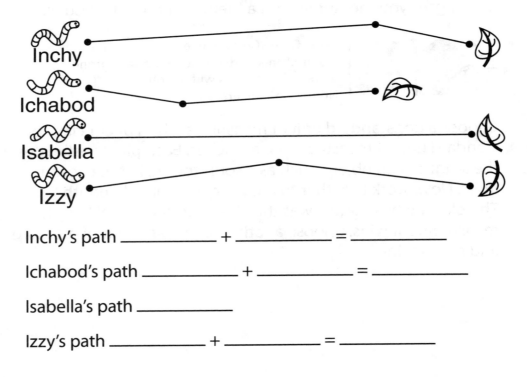

Inchy's path _____ + _____ = _____

Ichabod's path _____ + _____ = _____

Isabella's path _____

Izzy's path _____ + _____ = _____

Answers: 3 + 1 = 4 inches; 1 + 2 = 3 inches; 4 inches; 2 + 2 = 4 inches; Ichabod has the shortest path.

268   Cracking the First Grade

Charts and Graphs

It might surprise you that first graders love to graph! If you look around your child's classroom, you will probably find tally charts, pictographs, and bar graphs depicting every type of information under the sun that is relevant to a six- or seven-year-old. You will see representations showing the kids' favorite foods, what type of pets they have, information on their favorite hobbies, what mode of transportation they use to get to school, and everything else in between.

The challenge is to help kids work through and understand each step of the process of creating charts and graphs. In school, your child will learn to first pose a question, then collect information in a thorough way to answer the question, then find the best way to organize and display the information collected. Finally, your child will analyze the information to see how the question was answered. Once your child is comfortable with each of these steps, no question will be too large, no answer too small, and no amount of data too difficult for him or her to interpret!

First things first: Get a sense of what your kid already knows. Turn the page and tell your kid to Jump Right In!

Here's what you'll need for this lesson:
- *markers or crayons*
- *paper*
- *sidewalk chalk*

Feel free to read the questions aloud.

Jump Right In!

1. How many cows are on Hawkin's Farm?

Animals on Hawkin's Farm

Pigs	Sheep	Cows
卌 卌	卌 卌	卌 ||
		卌 卌	
	卌 卌	

A. 5 cows

B. 7 cows

C. 11 cows

D. 30 cows

2. How many pears are in the fruit bowl?

Fruit in the Fruit Bowl

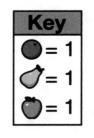

A. 1 pear

B. 2 pears

C. 3 pears

D. 4 pears

3. Complete the tally chart to show the number of each shape.

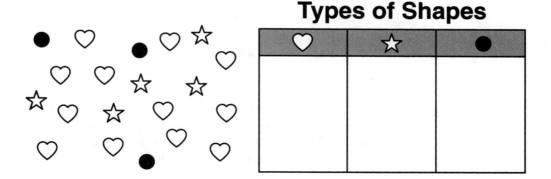

Types of Shapes

♡	☆	●

4. Use the graph to answer the questions.

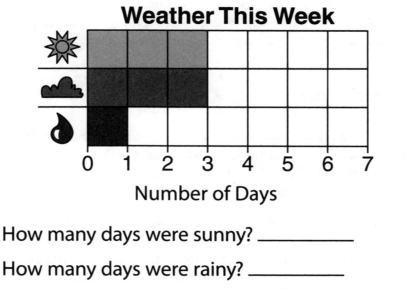

Weather This Week

Number of Days

How many days were sunny? _____

How many days were rainy? _____

How many more sunny days were there than rainy days? _____

 *Checking In*

Ⓐ Answers for pages 270 and 271:

    1. B

    2. B

    3. An A+ answer: 12 tallies for hearts, 5 tallies for stars, and 3 tallies for circles

    4. An A+ answer: 3, 1, and 2

Did your child get the correct answers? You could ask, "How did you know where to find the information you needed to answer the questions?" Let your child explain the charts and graphs to you. Use the charts and graphs to ask your child comparison questions. For example, for question 1, "What animal is there the most of?"

Did your child get one of the answers wrong? You might ask, "What type of information are you looking for?" or say, "Tell me what you did first." Help your child break down what he or she did into steps. For example, have your child ask herself, "What is it I need to find out?" and "What information is the graph showing me?" Help your child read the title of each graph, find appropriate columns, count tally marks (question 1), pictures (questions 2 and 3), or shaded boxes (question 4).

 *Watch Out!*

Children enjoy the process of making tally marks, but they sometimes get confused about how to organize and count them. Because of their work with the base-ten number system and place value, children are inclined to count each group of tally marks by tens, rather than fives.

Emphasize that each group of tally marks has five marks in it by having your child count each tally mark as he writes it. To remind your child to cross over four tally marks to show five tally marks, ask him to imagine that the tally marks are sticks or logs. Have your child draw four tally marks, then cross over the group with the fifth tally mark like making a bundle of five sticks or logs. Demonstrate for your child how to count the bundles by fives and any "leftover sticks" by ones.

Cracking the First Grade

What to Know...

Collecting and representing data using charts and graphs is a culmination of many of the skills your child is learning in first grade.

Review these skills with your child this way:

- A **tally** is a way of counting by making a mark for each item counted.
- A **tally chart** is a table that shows data with tally marks.

Your child could use a tally chart to keep track of neighborhood soccer game wins or wins and losses playing checkers with Dad.

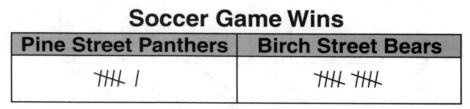

Soccer Game Wins

Pine Street Panthers	Birch Street Bears
‖‖ ‖	‖‖ ‖‖

Look at the tally chart with your child. Ask your child, "What information is shown by the chart? How many wins by the Panthers? How many by the Bears? Who has more wins? Who has less?" Make a tally chart with your child using information about your own family. For example, count the number of pairs of shoes each family member owns and represent the information using a tally chart.

- A **pictograph** is a graph that shows data by using picture symbols. Each pictograph has a key that tells how many items each symbol represents.

Your child could use a pictograph to show how many of each type of flower are in the garden.

Flowers in the Garden

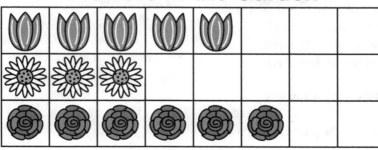

Key
🌷 = 1
🌼 = 1
🌹 = 1

Read the key and pictograph with your child. Use stickers or rubber stamps to make another pictograph of a collection of toys or items that are important to your child.

- A **bar graph** is a graph that shows data by using bars of different sizes.

Your child might use a bar graph to find out what snacks his classmates like best.

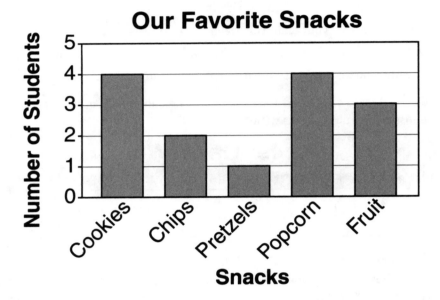

Read the bar graph with your child. Point out how the bars are longer or shorter depending on how many children chose each snack. Ask your child to add her choice for favorite snack on the graph by shading the appropriate square, and then explain how the bar graph changed.

 *Checking In*

Kids need to know that there is more to a graph than displaying data. They can use graphs and charts to answer questions. For example, a classroom graph might answer the question: How do the students get to school each day?

When using graphs and charts, make sure your child understands what question is being asked and answered. Be certain to help your child create a title for each graph or chart he or she constructs, and remind your kid to read the title on any graph or chart with which he or she is working.

First Graders Are...

First graders like to see their work displayed and are very proud of their accomplishments. What looks like some jumbled lines on a piece of paper to you might be their attempt at creating their own graph! Find an area in your home to display *all* the work that is important to your child. Respecting your kid's efforts, big and small, shows your child that the work he or she does is important to you too.

Your child can practice working with charts and graphs with these activities. You'll probably want to read these activities aloud to your child.

On Your Way to an "A" Activities

Type: Speaking/Listening
Materials needed: pencil, paper
Number of players: 3 or more

Did you ever wish you knew your friends and family better? Well, now is your chance! Think of some questions to ask them like, "What is your favorite color: red, orange, yellow, green, blue, or purple?" or "What is your favorite season: summer, fall, winter, or spring?" Make a tally chart for each question to display the answers. Share the results with your friends and family.

Type: Active
Materials needed: sidewalk chalk
Number of players: 1 or more

It's time for a nature walk outdoors! With someone in your house, collect items like leaves, wildflowers, or pebbles. You can even use your backyard if you'd like. Ask someone to help you draw a bar graph on the sidewalk or driveway with chalk. Graph how many of each type of item you collected. Don't forget to give each graph a title and to label the rows and columns on the graph.

Has your child breezed through the activities? If so, he or she can work on this Using Your Head activity independently. You may want to read the activity aloud to your child.

Using Your Head

{**20** minutes}

*Grab some **crayons** or **markers**!*

The animals are hiding in the rain forest. Can you find and graph them?

Animals in the Rain Forest

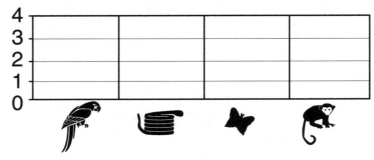

Answers: 4 macaws, 2 anacondas, 4 butterflies, 2 spider monkeys

Notes

Notes

Notes